Practical Guidelines for Integrated Quality Management in Tourism Destinations

Concepts, Implementation and Tools
for Destination Management Organizations

**Practical Guidelines for Integrated Quality Management in Tourism Destinations –
Concepts, Implementation and Tools for Destination Management Organizations**
ISBN (printed version):   978-92-844-1797-1
ISBN (electronic version): 978-92-844-1798-8

Published by the World Tourism Organization (UNWTO).
First printing: 2017
All rights reserved.
Printed in Spain.

The present publication is a translation into English from the Spanish original published in 2015 entitled *Manual práctico de gestión integral de la calidad de los destinos turísticos – Conceptos, implementación y herramientas para autoridades, instituciones y gestores de destinos.*

The designations employed and the presentation of material in this publication do not imply the expression of any opinions whatsoever on the part of the publishers concerning the legal status of any country, territory, city or area, or of its authorities or concerning the delimitation of its frontiers or boundaries.

World Tourism Organization (UNWTO)   Tel.: (+34) 915 678 100
Calle Capitán Haya, 42   Fax: (+34) 915 713 733
28020 Madrid   Website: www.unwto.org
Spain   E-mail: omt@unwto.org

Citation: *World Tourism Organization (2017), Practical Guidelines for Integrated Quality Management in Tourism Destinations – Concepts, Implementation and Tools for Destination Management Organizations, UNWTO, Madrid.*

Table of contents

Acknowledgments

This publication would not have been possible without the initiative of the Destination Management and Quality Programme of the World Tourism Organization (UNWTO) and the support of its Secretary-General, Mr. Taleb Rifai. Following the Organization's work in the field of tourism quality, the Programme seeks to update the knowledge, clarify the concepts and develop the basic tools for improving quality at tourism destinations.

This guide could not have been completed without the wide knowledge and experience in the field of tourism of a contributor to the project, Mr. Victor Gorga.

I wish to thank all of the members of the UNWTO Committee on Tourism and Competitiveness for dedicating their time and effort to reviewing the text of this publication. Their contributions were extremely valuable.

I also wish to thank the work of formal editing of the text conducted by Mrs. Nancy Cockerell and Mr. Antonio Rincón Córcoles.

My deepest appreciation goes to all who contributed to these *Practical Guidelines for Integrated Quality Management in Tourism Destinations,* and to you, our readers, for choosing it. We hope it will contribute to the improvement of quality performance at your destination.

Márcio Favilla
Executive Director,
Operational Programmes and Institutional Relations (UNWTO)

Preface

The publication of this handbook comes at a very opportune time, in the midst of a paradigm change in what is referred to as the quality of tourism destinations.

Quality is an increasingly important factor in the competitiveness of the tourism sector and long-term success of tourism destinations, since it has to do essentially with the satisfaction of visitor expectations.

In order to compete effectively in the global tourism market, destinations need to offer a unique experience and excellent value for their visitors. The quality of the experience is affected by a variety of public and private services, interactions with the local community, environment and hospitality and therefore requires an approach shared by all interested actors and the generation of public-private partnerships.

UNWTO defines the *quality of a tourism destination* as "the result of a process which implies the satisfaction of all tourism product and service needs, requirements and expectations of the consumer at an acceptable price, in conformity with mutually accepted contractual conditions and the implicit underlying factors such as safety and security, hygiene, accessibility, communication, infrastructure and public amenities and services. It also involves aspects of ethics, transparency and respect towards the human, natural and cultural environment". Aspects of quality also relate to ethics, transparency and respect for the human, natural and cultural environment.

These *Practical Guidelines for Integrated Quality Management in Tourism Destinations* outline a comprehensive and pragmatic approach to the quality of destinations, and the components that go into it, for use by decision-makers, managers, planners, academics, professionals and entrepreneurs. They clarify and reflect upon concepts with the aim of improving knowledge and learning from practical experience.

I am certain this publication will help destinations gain an in-depth and clear understanding of the framework for quality and how to use the tools needed to improve quality and ensure the competitive development of the sector.

Taleb Rifai
Secretary-General,
World Tourism Organization (UNWTO)

Part one
Key concepts

Chapter 1

The concept of quality in tourism

Summary   This chapter defines the scope of the term quality, which, though commonly used, is subject to different interpretations and applications – all correct and complementary – as a result of a process in which objective, as well as subjective elements intervene.

Key words
- Quality;
- Expectations;
- Perceptions; and
- Competitiveness.

Key message   As a key factor in the competitiveness of tourism destinations, quality is a criterion as well as an approach to work based on how effective management is conceived, considering the social, environmental and economic effects of tourism activity as judged, ultimately, in terms of customer satisfaction.

The methodology used to apply quality to tourism is determined by the distinguishing characteristics of tourism itself (interaction, simultaneity of production and consumption, sale of existential and symbolic utilities, intangibility of many of its components, heterogeneity), as well as by the coordination of relevant actors at the destination.

In the context of tourism, quality is something that derives from an intimate personal experience. It is more than a chain of technically sound activities; it represents an ethical choice with implications for sustainability, social responsibility, accessibility, and fair trade.

The benefits of attending to quality are obvious, for visitors, businesses, destinations and residents. It is a choice from which everyone gains.

1.1   The concept of quality in tourism

Over time it has become clear that the introduction of quality assurance reference models and systems is not a passing fashion. Quality has become a necessary ingredient for organizations and tourism destinations seeking to gain recognition in the market, locally, nationally or globally.

Today it is a factor that influences competitiveness and a characteristic that visitors appreciate and demand.

In the context of tourism, quality does not consist only of producing "zero defects" and meeting basic requisites; it also signifies care, innovation and excellence. It is not merely a matter of meeting customer expectations but of surpassing them. What is required in the case of a business is the committed leadership of management; for a tourism destination, it is a matter of achieving the critical mass needed to be representative of, and foster commitment and coordination among, the public and private entities concerned.

Quality is an intrinsic aspect of any good, product or service. It is a common factor that defines commonly accepted social standards. It is therefore logical that the term should be used so often, and to mean such varied things.

In the literature on quality and quality assurance in practice, this concept needs to be interpreted with reference to one or more of the following key points:

1. In its most *transcendent* meaning, as a synonym for excellence, it is a philosophical approach that cannot be defined but only appreciated. When considered from a material standpoint, it is associated with price, exclusivity, top-of-the-line supply and, to some extent, luxury. It is frequently used to indicate products for the high income market segments;

2. As a synonym for a *client-centred approach,* the concept of quality relates to the degree of satisfaction and the extent to which services and products meet customer expectations and needs. In this usage, quality is a subjective term and may be perceived differently for any given product, service or client;

3. As a term specifying the *characteristics of a product or service,* quality takes on a more precise meaning that is recognizable and measurable and allows for objective ranking, as in the case of hotel classification;

4. With reference to *production processes,* quality is understood in more technical terms, as a system or set of practices necessary to bring a product or service in line with applicable standards. In that sense, quality represents a tool for improving management; and

5. As an *economic* term, quality is defined in terms of product characteristics, production costs and sales price. Mentally, tourists link price, category and quality, so they will be ready to pay a reasonable supplement for a product if its quality is superior.

Each of these often coexisting interpretations refers to a fundamental, complementary and equally valid aspect of quality.

1.1.1 Quality has different dimensions

The definitions set out above are all to some extent imprecise when it comes to identifying the elements that make a product or service a *quality* product or service.

When it comes to evaluating a customer's satisfaction, the customer has needs and expectations in respect of a series of characteristics, tangible and intangible. In the case of largely functional products, such as air transport, aspects such as comfort, service, duration, connectivity, timetables, frequency of flights, etc. shape perceptions and carry greater weight in the choice of airline and purchase of tickets.

In the case of less technical products, as well as most services, which are often undifferentiated until they are consumed, the perception of quality is associated with intangible and aesthetic components. For products that consist of an experience, such as tourism packages and destinations, the intangible components are generally the ones that can create a strategic advantage. Brand image, the manner in which a service is provided or recommendations (by travel critics, family members or in the social networks) all shape the customer's perception.

The quality of a tourism product or service is experienced in a highly subjective way, as a function of expectations and perceptions that are difficult to isolate. Both must be continuously considered to understand the quality processes of a service.

The SERVQUAL[1] model assesses the quality of a service as the sum of five dimensions:

1. In terms of its weight in generating satisfaction, the *physical component* represents barely 10%, while the other four dimensions – those concerned, by order of importance, with *accordance, response capacity, reliability and empathy* – together represent 90%;

2. *Accordance* is the degree to which the technical aspects, such as the knowledge and skills of service personnel, meet the standards specified, contributing to credibility and confidence;

3. *Response capacity* refers to willingness, promptness, competence and courtesy in solving client problems;

4. *Reliability* refers to the ability to provide standardized service in a reliable and conscientious manner to follow through on the "sales promise"; and

5. Lastly, and with a weight slightly greater than that attributed to the physical component, is *empathy,* the individualized attention offered to each customer which, while of equal important cannot balance out or replace a lack of professionalism, consistency or deficiency in management.

1.1.2   Defining and interpreting quality

Customers are the ones who establish their level of satisfaction by returning to buy more. Quality means giving customers what they want at the lowest possible cost. It seems like a simple definition but embodies two seemingly opposing precepts. The first ("giving customers what they want") calls for a client-oriented approach; the second ("at the lowest possible cost") calls for effective, competitive and profitable management.

Quality therefore represents three things at once:

–   *A professional tool;*

–   *A management model;* and

–   *A powerful marketing tool.*

Figure 1.1   **Quality as a balance between expectations and satisfaction**

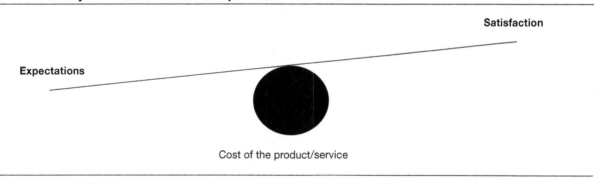

As a *professional tool,* quality is achieved by knowing and controlling general, as well as specific processes for delivering services profitably.

1   Parasuraman, A.; Zeithaml, V. A. and Berry, L. L. (1988), 'SERVQUAL a Multiple-Item Scale for Measuring Consumer Perceptions of Service Quality', *Journal of Retailing,* volume 64 (1), Spring.

Quality systematization involves three different levels of action:

1. *Organizational,* including awareness and commitment, development of procedures and planning;
2. *Operational,* to permit continuous improvement with the help of tools and based on continuous performance review; and
3. *Perceptual* (in terms of market recognition) which represents a strategic and commercial variable verified through the market by the work of audit firms and certification agencies and recognized and esteemed by means of prestige or conformity marks.

In tourism, quality necessarily involves the active commitment of human resources. In the case of destinations, it also requires a spirit of hospitality among local residents.

As a *management model* quality rests on a new framework of working relationships and competencies. This means moving from a pyramidal, silo structure to a flat, process-orientated organization. In the case of a destination, it requires solid public-private and inter-institutional commitments.

As a *marketing and loyalty-creating tool* quality puts the customer at the centre of activities, which implies knowing and paying attention to the customer's needs, which is also an objective of marketing.

Quality standards and related branding are designed to facilitate international commercial exchanges by recognizing the characteristics of products, services and companies in terms of common, accepted standards.

The World Tourism Organization (UNWTO) introduced *quality of tourism services* as part of its work programme in 1991, *at that time* defining it "as the result of a process that implies satisfaction of every need, request or rightful expectation of consumers in respect of products and services, at an acceptable price, and under mutually agreed contractual conditions, including implicit underlying factors like hygiene, accessibility, authenticity and concerns about the human and natural environmental consequences of the tourism activities."[2]

If we analyse every word of this definition, we come to understand that quality:

- Cannot exist without the harmonious and active participation of all the factors that contribute to the tourist's experience;
- Must result from constant effort to limit the activity's deficiencies and failures;
- Is fundamentally and directly related to the activity's human and personal dimensions, which are mainly intangible and thus largely subjective;
- Responds to a fair price as an exchange for fulfilling basic and vital needs of people, which is determined by social and environmental limits;
- Requires common and irrevocable criteria and the convergence of mandatory requirements and self-regulation;
- Incorporates rights for both final and intermediate consumers governed by contracts or transparent mechanisms regarding promotion;

---

2   World Tourism Organization (2003), *UNWTO Quality Support Committee at its sixth meeting,* Varadero, Cuba, 9–10 May 2003, UNWTO, Madrid.

- Results, in the case of a destination, from collective effort; and
- Cannot be judged solely from the perspective of customer satisfaction, but also in terms of the activity's social, economic and environmental effects.

UNWTO nowadays defines *quality of a tourism destination* as "the result of a process which implies the satisfaction of all tourism product and service needs, requirements and expectations of the consumer at an acceptable price, in conformity with mutually accepted contractual conditions and the implicit underlying factors such as safety and security, hygiene, accessibility, communication, infrastructure and public amenities and services. It also involves aspects of ethics, transparency and respect towards the human, natural and cultural environment."[3]

It can therefore be concluded that quality should form part of management, as well as planning, with the ultimate aim of improving performance and characterizing and adapting the supply of products and services, strengthening competitive variables for the destination.

1.1.3 What is different about applying the concept of quality to tourism?

Tourism combines a series of particular characteristics that differentiate it from other productive services and which contribute to and affect the development and implementation of quality:
- Interaction between providers and customers at the production level;
- Simultaneous production and consumption;
- Sale of existential and symbolic utilities;
- Intangible components; and
- Heterogeneity.

Delivery of the tourism product requires a contribution from customers. These are products in which personal experience plays a large part. The immediacy between production and consumption makes for unusual intensity in the customer-provider-destination relationship and numerous "moments of truth" when the visitor's overall assessment is largely subjective and conditioned by circumstances, personal habits and travel experience, as well as by the preconceived ideas and expectations generated during the travel planning process based on previously gathered opinions and information.

Fatigue after a long journey or emotion over starting an anxiously awaited holiday, can create a state of mind that affects how any purchased service is perceived. For a tour operator or destination, the simultaneity of production and consumption reduces control over processes; there is no time to correct mistakes, hence the importance of "doing it right the first time".

---

3   This is the UNWTO definition of "Quality of a tourism destination" which was endorsed by the 103 UNWTO Executive Council held in Málaga, Spain, in May 2016, and which has been introduced in the present English version. By the time the Spanish version of this publication was released in 2015 this definition could not be included.

1.2   Links between quality and other fields

Quality, going beyond an integrated process of technically solvent performance, is an ethical option. Responsibility and an attitude of doing things well and respecting both people and the environment are matters of ethics. Here is where quality, sustainability, social responsibility, accessibility and fair trade all come together. There can be no quality without ethics.

Quality in tourism is inherent to the intimate sphere of the person. In tourism we sell not only functional but also experiential, emotional and symbolic utilities. This exceeds the usual concept of a consumer product and gives tourism an important moral dimension. Material purchases can be refunded or changed, but the experience of not having quality in tourism cannot. This is what makes the tourism product so delicate and special: tourist dissatisfaction is very difficult to rectify.

In that sense, a destination that tolerates inequality, prostitution or abusive trade, or that does not protect local heritage, or where activities are not planned on a sustainable basis, irrespective of how attractive its resources might be, cannot be considered a quality destination.

Quality interacts with other areas of concern that are related to tourism: sustainability and accessibility.

1.2.1   Sustainability as an attribute of quality

The main attraction of a destination is the environment, natural or urban, and its deterioration is the first and most evident cause of dissatisfaction for tourists.

Sustainability shares the same principles as quality because tourism requires long-term strategies and uses finite resources that are highly sensitive to deterioration, such as nature and human heritage, without which tourist interest and motivation disappear.

The social, cultural, economic and environmental sustainability of tourism activities is a component of quality in tourism, and, at the same time, a guarantee of business survival. Moreover, sustainability is an ethical responsibility, together with quality, and a competitive variable. It is therefore unsurprising to see the two concepts closely related, particularly in managing destinations.

Case study 1.1   **Green Globe Programme**

Green Globe is an initiative dating back to the United Nations Earth Summit in 1992. It was supported at that time by 19 tourism associations which by 1995 had grown to some 350 members in 74 countries.

In 1997, in parallel with its programme for enterprises Green Globe launched a programme for destinations, based on Agenda 21 criteria with pilot programmes in Vilamoura (Portugal), Jersey (United Kingdom) and Crete and Corfu (Greece). Green Globe certification was introduced in 2002 with the participation of accredited certification bodies.

The programme was revitalized in 2008, when it was purchased by Green Globe International Inc., a publicly-owned company from the United States of America.

Green Globe evaluates a series of indicators based on four criteria: planning and management for sustainable development, impact on socioeconomic development, management and promotion of cultural heritage and care for the environment and resources.

1.2.2   Accessibility as an attribute of quality

The World Health Organization (WHO)[4] defines disability as a "restriction or lack of capacity to be able to do daily activities" and it classifies it in three different groups: intellectual, physical and sensory. Not all disabilities are pathological: accident victims, pregnant women and the elderly all require special attention during travel.

The WHO *Global Report on Disability*[5] estimates that more than 1 billion people live with some kind of disability throughout the world, representing about 15% of global population. Therefore, attending to their needs, apart from considerations of solidarity, means considering a defined market segment, in some cases subsidized or with high purchasing power, in which potential demand still far exceeds supply.

The Manila Declaration on World Tourism[6] for the first time recognised tourism as a fundamental right and an element in human and social development, and accessibility as an indispensable requirement for quality in tourism.

1.3   Quality in tourism as a factor to competitiveness

The need to ensure excellent service as the final result strengthens the conviction that maximum consistency and uniformity should be ensured in service delivery, which can happen only if quality management systems are applied. Quality is managed. It does not happen by itself. Quality achieved through management, still understood by many as "value added", is a matter of competitiveness if not survival.

Investments in quality must be considered in medium- to long-term time frames; implementing a quality system requires effort (not least in overcoming resistance to change), monitoring, time, and money – costs that can be significant in the early stages. But when it becomes part of the everyday process, less effort is required and the returns easily surpass the initial cost.

Consequently, in contending with consolidated ones, emerging destinations, free of inertia and bad habits, gain a competitive advantage when they correctly plan their tourism activity.

1.3.1   Benefits of quality for the tourist

Quality provides three basic advantages to tourism customers:
1.   Quality in the design phase of products, packages and services assures *adaptation to the customer's needs and expectations;*
2.   When buying, quality *reduces the uncertainty* that travel generates. Customers may buy with confidence, even without previous experience of the destination and there is a time gap between the moment of the purchase and the moment of consumption; and

---

4   World Health Organization (1980), *International Classification of Impairments, Disabilities, and Handicaps: Manual for classifying the consequences,* WHO, Geneva.

5   World Health Organization (2011), *World report on disability 2011,* WHO, Geneva.

6   World Tourism Organization (1980), *Manila Declaration on World Tourism,* UNWTO, Manila.

3. Finally, quality generates confidence in the response capacity of the provider, a *guarantee* of professionalism and after-sales attention. One should remember that the tourist, outside his or her usual environment, is the most vulnerable partner in this contract, especially when travel has emotional or professional importance or involves unfamiliar cultures or languages.

1.3.2   Benefits of quality for companies

By focusing their attention on customers, an emphasis on quality will help companies design better products and services, better adapted to demand and therefore generating greater acceptance and differentiating them more from others, improving sales and building loyalty. Quality also allows for higher prices.

There are other, far from negligible benefits for companies, linked to management, internal commitment and image refinement:
– The work environment is improved: professionalization and clarity in the distribution of tasks and identification, commitment and convergence of objectives among collaborators and providers;
– Efficiency is increased, as reflected among other things in a reduction of so-called non-quality costs, which often represent up to a third of total billing; and
– Company negotiating positions in relation to other components in the value chain will be strengthened, since quality, when certified, constitutes a complementary instrument for promotion and marketing.

Finally, in terms of customer satisfaction the inevitable connection between the quality of a destination and the quality of the companies operating there is well proven.

1.3.3   Benefits of quality for the destination

Quality initiatives also produce benefits, though less immediately visible, for destinations and even local societies:
– They improve a destination's image and positioning;
– They increase its capacity to compete against other destinations;
– They guarantee a stronger position for destinations in their high-pressure contract negotiations with operators;
– They involve agents and other industry partners, contributing to a stronger, more cohesive business environment;
– They bring substantial changes to management and planning;
– They offer an effective alternative to enacted legislation;
– They generate direct benefits for local communities; and
– They allow a significant share of implementation and monitoring costs to be transferred, reducing the financial burden for taxpayers.

1.4   International perspectives on the quality of tourism

Tourism has pioneered the application of quality to a quintessentially tertiary sector, often by extrapolating from experience. Once clearly defined technical processes for service delivery (the what) have been developed and consolidated, as for the hotel sector for instance, it has proven useful to understand which aspects may have a negative impact on the delivery of those services, what is called functional quality (the how).

Awareness about the need to approach quality in tourism as a competitive strategy increased in the early 1990s, as a consequence of the economic crisis that followed the First Gulf War. It seems to have led to two different tendencies: the development of an internal quality culture, starting within company management and later spreading to destination management; and the use of tools to improve internal and external communication with customers, to identify their needs and to focus the company's attention on trends in demand, though not as part of a real business strategy or commitment to customers.

Though still incipient, quality is a matter of growing concern in the tourism sector. Given its complexity, however, it is often approached from contradictory or self-interested perspectives, which make it difficult to understand and implement on a widespread basis.

So while some companies take advantage of the effort involved in implementing quality to reposition or restructure their businesses in terms of management and human resources, to increase productivity, and to improve the efficiency and quality of services, others exhibit *quality* as an internal and external sales argument, but as a merely cosmetic improvement, without making any real and profound improvements to their activities.

The number of countries that have introduced mandatory classification and categorization systems, with the implicit or explicit aim of indicating a determined level of quality, has been increasing. In some cases these systems coexist alongside self-regulation and commercial branding systems. These systems are intended to bring order to growing supply and fill the legal gaps that affect various tourism subsectors, services or products, particularly those associated with active tourism, in emerging destinations.

In parallel with national efforts, various international committees, particularly those of the International Standardization Organization (ISO), work to harmonize the already numerous and dispersed standardization initiatives for the sector under a single regulatory umbrella.

While great progress has been made in recent years in the standardization and certification of products, companies and people, case studies referring to the comprehensive management of destinations have been fewer and farther between.

A number of current studies suggest that priority is being given in the short term to improving communication, benchmarking, and business collaboration, together with human resources programmes to strengthen relationships and promote initiative and experimentation. However, with the entry of investor groups without a tradition in tourism, the industry generally seems to have opted instead for leadership in prices or costs and strategies for accelerated business expansion or concentration.

Chapter 2

Quality and the customer

Summary   This chapter deals with quality as a process of interaction between activities planned by organizations and the expectations and perceptions of different tourism customers.

Key words
- Customers;
- Needs, expectations and demand;
- Programmed quality, realized quality, expected quality, perceived quality, objective quality;
- Quality gaps; and
- Loyalty-creation.

Key message   Quality management revolves around the concept of customers and their satisfaction as a priority, understanding and attending to their needs and expectations. The customers of tourism activity consist not only of visitors but also of businesspersons, suppliers and residents.

The level of customer satisfaction is a first way to measure quality, though imprecise, constantly changing and subjective. The absence of complaints, however, does not signify satisfaction. Room for improvement in the space between expectations and satisfaction is referred to as quality gaps, which any quality system seeks to reduce. Achieving excellence means meeting or surpassing the expectations created. What is important is inducing customers to return and recommend the experience to others.

Handling complaints is one of the areas in which failure is most common. A complaint that is properly handled represents an invaluable opportunity for improvement and loyalty creation.

2.1   The customer

Quality management revolves around the concept of customers and their satisfaction as a priority, understanding and attending to their needs and expectations. It is an approach that needs to be shared and that entails dealing adequately with certain technical aspects in order to be successful.

The management of customer satisfaction requires actors at the destination, as well as tour operators in generating markets to commit to and take responsibility for the design of travel programmes, proposed improvements for the destination and the local delivery of services, even those provided by third parties. In the same way, everything that happens to the customer or components in the value chain will affect the destination's image.

Figure 2.1   **Customers and approaches to tourism**

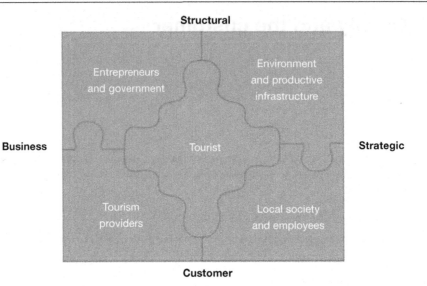

In the case of tourism, the term *customer* refers to visitors but also to:
–   *Entrepreneurs* (and the government), who seek returns from their investments and recognition for their initiatives;
–   *Providers* who form part of the chain for delivery of the service;
–   *Local society,* which seeks to obtain direct or indirect returns from tourism, at least in terms of employment;
–   The *environment* and *heritage* that needs to be preserved in the interests of business continuity; and
–   *Productive infrastructure,* which requires maintenance.

All of these customers must be dealt with in the destination's quality plan, which must therefore bring together the following four theoretical approaches to quality:
1.   A *client-focused* approach, consisting of loyalty initiatives, improvements in the migration process, the dissemination of security protocols, the prevention of risks associated with food security and health, and the transparency, accessibility and sufficiency of information made available to visitors;
2.   An *entrepreneurial* approach, entailing investment in training, the development of competencies, job security, company professionalization, the promotion of private initiative, or the certification of persons;
3.   A *structural* approach, including mechanisms for public-private management, measures to support the maintenance and upgrading of tourism infrastructure, and the implementation of environmental and social programmes; and
4.   A *strategic* approach might consist of a proposal for positioning and planning designed to achieve profitable returns from the business, a concerted development model agreed to among actors at the destination and mechanisms to preserve and strengthen tourism assets and heritage.

Countries where tourism is more consolidated consider various models for tourism planning and transformation, as well as programmes for the updating of tourism supply, the renewal of assets, professionalization, excellence or marketing.

Case study 2.1 **Acapulco Modernization Plan (Mexico)**

Acapulco (Mexico), which was a fashionable destination and at the forefront of Pacific sun and beach tourism from the 1940s to the 1970s, entered into decline for lack of urban planning, which was clearly evident in its indiscriminate construction, overpopulation, illegal occupation of land, unequal and exclusive development, insecurity and inadequate basic services, including sanitation, which ultimately polluted the beaches. In 1997, Hurricane Paulina devastated Acapulco, taking 400 lives, injuring 10,000 and causing unquantifiable material damage.

At the end of the 1990s the Mexican government took several measures to regenerate beaches and reorganize and revitalize the destination.

In 2002, the Sectoral Plan for Tourism Development in Greater Acapulco outlined a series of urban development measures and steps to reposition the destination. These were carried out between 2003 and 2015, in a joint effort by the state of Guerrero, FONATUR and the municipalities of Acapulco, Juárez and Coyuca de Benítez, under the management of a public-private consortium: the Commission for Development of Greater Acapulco (CODEMA).

Funded with more than USD 400 million, the plan had the objectives of re-establishing environmental conditions and improving urban conditions in order to promote sustainable development of the area, develop areas with the greatest potential for tourism development and improve and diversify tourism supply.

The plan provided for activities in eight key areas:

1.   Zoning;

2.   New access facilities;

3.   Better facilities and services;

4.   Enhanced mobility;

5.   Reduced pollution;

6.   Water treatment;

7.   New tourism infrastructure; and

8.   Expansion and updating of current supply.

2.1.1 Difference between needs, wishes and expectations

There is no perfect product or destination that will satisfy all customers.

Quality in the sense of customer satisfaction is built according to customers' needs, not their latest whims or demands, which can go in and out of fashion. A common mistake among organizations and destinations is to shift the quality focus from attending to customers' needs and expectations to pursue their latest *wish lists*. Hygiene, security or accessibility, for instance, fall in the first category; digital information points fall in the second, since what is *needed* can be provided by other means.

Planning and purchasing a trip to a destination implies a series of customer expectations. To meet expectations, which combine the *need to have* with the *wish to have* we must first focus on needs.

Customer expectations are generated by a combination of aspirations, mental images (iconography), promotional information, recommendations, competitor behaviour and the customer's travel experience, motivations and available resources.

Customer dissatisfaction results from bad experiences at the destination as well as failures to live up to expectations, which are often unrealistically high.

2.1.2   Visitor satisfaction as a measure of quality

Customer satisfaction allows us to establish a preliminary measure of quality, but one that is imprecise, because it is associated, as we have seen, with subjective expectations.

It is possible to obtain a high number of satisfied customers if expectations are low. This is what happens in destinations that, despite having compelling tourism attractions, do not offer enough information about the destination and complementary products or activities. Tourists sometimes lower their own expectations as a safeguard against disappointment. Artificially inflated expectations, on the other hand, can lead to dissatisfaction at the best of destinations.

Similarly, the absence of complaints is not synonymous with satisfaction, just as indifference is not the same as dissatisfaction.

A more precise measure has to do with the destination's prescriptive capacity: intention to return, recommendation, reputation.

Recommendations clearly represent a qualitative measure of satisfaction, since when customers get what they want, have requested and paid for they do not feel any need to communicate the fact, as they would if not satisfied. Dissatisfied customers tend to communicate their experience to at least three times as many people as satisfied customers do. Various studies show that the medium-term cost of dealing with a dissatisfied customer is on average six times greater than the cost of attracting a new customer, counting all of the costs of attending to the problem or complaint, compensating the customer and the damage done in terms of image.

According to various studies, an average of 96% of customers do not communicate their complaints, but simply choose different providers or destinations the next time, while always sharing their dissatisfaction with people they know. Research has shown that a satisfied consumer shares his or her experience with an average of six people, while a dissatisfied customer does so with at least 11. Nowadays, if they also make their complaints public via social networks the impact is unpredictable

The reason for not expressing their dissatisfaction may be associated with a lack of confidence in the response capacity of the provider, who is thus deprived of the information needed to improve. In the case of destinations the problem is even worse, since the person responsible for dealing with customers in a destination, unlike an organization, is not identifiable.

How complaints are dealt with is probably the most common problem in customer service. From the time the customer perceives the problem up to the time it becomes a serious threat to the viability of the destination or organization, the tourist goes through several states of mind, ranging from emotional to rational. If an incident is resolved quickly, between 82% and 95% of the customers having complained about it return. In only 1% of non-quality situations is the relationship with the customer irrecoverable. A complaint is the best opportunity to improve matters and, if adequately addressed, can increase customer loyalty.

It can be estimated, based on the costs of attracting a new customer, that a complaint can cost anywhere from around USD 1,370 to USD 15,000, depending on how far the negative information has penetrated through to potential customers.

2.1.3   Loyalty-creation

The objective in creating loyalty is to transform occasional customers into regular customers, and these into promoters. Various studies have shown that recommendations are the most important source of guidance in making purchases (44%), as compared to others under the control of providers: the media (25%), advertising (24%), direct selling and other sources (7%).

Destinations, as well as providers can also cultivate customer loyalty. Captive demand nurtured developed in this way can be an asset for some destinations: the European Union's Eurobarometre, which measures the attractiveness of major tourism destinations for Europeans and their and intention to visit them, always ranks Italy, France or Spain among the top choices.

2.2   Quality from the customer's perspective

2.2.1   Perception of different levels of quality

Customers perceive the quality of services in an individualized, subjective and evolving manner. Such perceptions differ from those derived from measuring and verifying processes objectively.

In order for customers to experience quality or excellence in services, their created expectations must be surpassed. Quality can thus be measured in terms of the difference between customers' expectations about a service and their perceptions of it once received. This requires the identification and evaluation of differences ('gaps') between the different quality levels, to be minimized through a system of continuous improvement with the goal of zero-defect service.

Quality levels are determined by the objectives of an organization or destination (programmed quality), internal measurements of progress toward those objectives (realized quality), customer expectations (expected quality) and perceptions about the components of a product's quality (perceived quality) as a final measure of satisfaction.

The intersection between expected and delivered or perceived quality is what we call "objective quality". Achieving objective quality is the purpose of any systematic quality management programme.

On the other hand, providers' or destinations' efforts that are not valued by customers, and that are derived from a mistaken interpretation of needs and expectations, are defined as "superfluous quality". Far from being appreciated by customers, they generate unnecessary costs and are difficult to produce consistently. They can even be a cause of dissatisfaction. Hotels, for example, as a result of the recent crisis in the sector, have reviewed and discontinued many unnecessary amenities – chocolates, newspapers, gifts, etc. – which are clear examples of superfluous quality.

2.2.2   When and how does a deficiency in service quality appear?

If customers' needs and expectations were always stable over time organizations and destinations could just achieve excellence in quality and maintain it indefinitely. But that is not how it works. Each customer's perceptions and expectations are different and always changing, depending on mood, external factors, value received for the price paid and actual consumption of the product. There is also the association phenomenon, in which a surprise feature of one product or service generates expectations about others.

While expectations are generic, higher priority tends to be given to some aspects of quality over others, depending on the type of tourism or service and the market segment concerned. For example, younger tourists, anxious to experience life and more willing to sacrifice comfort, are also more sensitive to such aspects as sustainability. Families, on the other hand, prefer destinations offering activities for all age groups and guaranteeing security. The senior segment appreciates comfort and is more inclined to travel to certain destinations based on travel company, climate, language, or available assistance. The business tourist values such aspects as accessibility, mobility at the destination and professional service; holiday travellers appreciate information, uncrowded attractions, professional guides, reasonable prices for excursions to tourism attractions, etc. For meetings industry tourism the destination's attractiveness, the adequacy of space and security are essential. For rural tourism, assistance, sign posting, hospitality, and supply of local activities are the prime considerations.

Gaps are mismatches between planning, expectations and perceptions, fundamental aspects of customer satisfaction; their measurement will establish the scope of action for efforts to improve. Basic steps to reduce such gaps include segmenting the market and understanding which attributes are most appreciated by customers, as well as their current perceptions and satisfaction levels.

The most important quality gaps result from three causes:
1.   Not knowing what users actually expect;
2.   Faulty or non-existent standards for work goals and performance, or lack of commitment; and
3.   Poor delivery.

Information communicated through the media, social networks and discussion groups can be a powerful influence in creating expectations. The publication of imprecise or inaccurate information generates expectations that can exceed the user's actual experience.

Chapter 3

Standardization of tourism quality

Summary   This chapter deals with the differences between standardization, certification and categorization.

Key words   – Standardization;
                     – Certification; and
                     – Categorization.

Key message   Standardization, certification and categorization are parallel but not synonymous concepts.

                     Standardization is the definition of operational or product specifications. When transformed into norms their purpose is to facilitate trade. Certification is public recognition that a company, product, process or person meets the requisites for a norm.

                     Categorization in tourism is a mechanism that combines standardization and certification but with a differentiating characteristic: it is an obligatory process, whereas quality standardization is usually and essentially a voluntary process.

3.1   Standardization, certification and categorization

Standardization, certification and categorization are parallel but not synonymous concepts.

Figure 3.1   **Differences between standardization, certification and categorization**

Standardization	Certification	Categorization
– Self-regulated/mandatory;	– Generally voluntary;	– Mandatory;
– Defines technical specifications;	– A form of recognition;	– Administrative requisite;
– Generally a participatory process;	– Market-oriented;	– Supported by a standard;
– Market/needs-oriented; and	– Supported by a standard;	– Exclusively technical approach;
– Public service/market oriented.	– Externally, independently validated;	– Organizational purpose; and
	– Commercial orientation; and	– Supervised by a public entity.
	– Associated with a brand.	

3.1.1   Standardization

Nowadays, standards are needed for any organized activity. Standardization is intended to establish solutions in repetitive situations by developing, disseminating and adopting uniform criteria.

One of the consequences of globalization is that productive processes worldwide are standardized, so that every company that wants to make incursions into a foreign market has to conform to internationally recognized standards to be accepted. Administered officially, the objective of standardization is to create reference points for producers and customers as to commercial processes in response to market demand. Standardization provides guidance in relation to a geographical, functional or even abstract area (e.g. symbols, terminology, testing procedures). Internationally standardized signposting for tourists is a good example.

In the case of companies, as well as destinations it is a process of defining operational or product specifications.

We standardize processes, products and services on a voluntary or mandatory, internal or external basis to validate and assure their quality; protect consumers, public health and the environment; promote the efficiency of organizations; and facilitate commercial exchange. Whether it be a self-regulated or mandatory process depends on how critical the need is: from the standpoint of sanitation, having a food hygiene system may be a basic mandatory requirement, whereas standardizing the quality of restaurant service is not.

Particularly when part of a self-regulated process, standards are established by committees composed of authorities, specialists, industry representatives and consumer representatives; they are subsequently subjected to public consultation prior to final publication.

3.1.2   Certification

In addition, as a mechanism for recognizing compliance with standards, we certify companies (management systems in particular), products, processes (e.g. for food hygiene) and people (qualifications and training).

Quality certification, which is always an external process, is the procedure – also known as as auditing – by which an accredited entity issues a written guarantee that a product, process or service is in accordance with specified requirements for either an official standard or one established for membership in a product club or use of a brand. Certification has an endorsing effect for customers and is thus a commercial initiative.

Certification is generally associated with what are called guarantee marks or conformity marks that certified entities can display publicly in support of their communication and promotion activities.

Figure 3.2   **Types of certification**

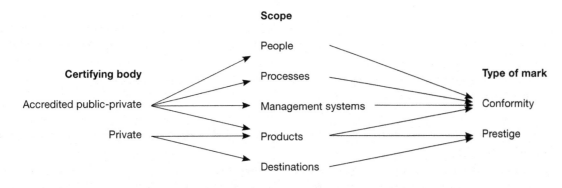

Obviously, any company or destination that needs to validate conformity with a standard will need certification. Since the certification of quality is a strategic decision and not a market imperative, and thus a means not an end, it can represent a competitive advantage if understood as a guarantee for the customer about the characteristics of the services purchased.

In some countries, the absence of reference standards allows tourism enterprises to self-certify their category. Many hotel chains unofficially evaluate and categorize their own hotels according to their own criteria and branding.

Destinations also self-certify. In Spain, those participating in the Comprehensive Destination Quality Model (SICTED) need first to undergo evaluation by accredited auditors participating in the implementation of quality at other destinations adhering to the model.

We only have true certification, however, when issued by an independent third party acting as guarantor. The job of confirming conformity with internal requisites developed by the entity being audited, or of reviewing external requisites, needs to be done by a disinterested organization.

Tour operators certify internal requisites to evaluate the quality of their providers, but conformity with a standard is almost always certified by third parties.

Certifiers include officially recognised entities (such as AENOR (see note on page 125 – List of acronyms and abbreviations), SGS, TÜV and Lloyds); official bodies (Eden destinations or EMAS in the European Union, Starlight, Creative Cities, UNESCO World Heritage Sites) and private sector players: clubs (tourism product clubs or routes), associations (Slow Cities) or companies (TripAdvisor, AAA, etc.).

Most certifications are public or private initiatives carried out by independent entities. Such is the case of Spains Tourism Quality System, a public promotion programme whose certification is entrusted to the Spanish Tourism Quality Institute, an independent, subsidized institution.

Case study 3.1   **Asociación Española de Normalización – AENOR (Spain)**

AENOR *(Asociación Española de Normalización* – Spanish Association for Standardisation and Certification) is a private non-profit institution and the body legally responsible for developing and disseminating technical standards in Spain. It is also a certification entity.

It has been linked to the Spanish Tourism Quality System from the start, supporting internationalization of the system and representing Spain on international standardization committees.

Together with Tunez, it leads Technical Committee ISO/TC 228, on Tourism and Related Services. It was created in 2005 and is currently composed of 83 countries, including active members and observers, and 13 associated organizations, including UNWTO and the European Union.

The Committee has published 20 standards to date with respect to diving, thalassotherapy, natural protected areas, adventure tourism, recreational ports, tourist information offices and beaches. All standards incorporate definitions to facilitate their use, as well as requisites and recommendations to improve the delivery of tourism services.

Note: In 2017, the activities of AENOR (Asociación Española de Normalización) have been divided into two bodies: (1) The Asociación Española de Normalización – UNE (Spanish Association for Stardardisation), carrying out standardisation and certification activities; and (2) AENOR, a commercial entity which works in the field of conformity assessment and other related areas, such as training and the sales of publications.

3.1.3   Categorization

Standardization and certification firms regulate tourism markets in many countries, under agreements with national governments.

An example of this is hotel categorization, a mechanism that combines standardization and certification but with an important difference: the process is mandatory, whereas quality standardization is usually voluntary.

Standardization differs from categorization as to objectives and application: while standards are intended to establish conditions for being considered satisfactory, categorization is a process of organizing and classifying supply according to different levels, sometimes using criteria that are more administrative than commercial.

Case study 3.2   **Tourism Grading Council (South Africa)**

Since its inception, the publicly-supported Tourism Grading Council of South Africa (TGCSA) has evolved from an ambitious programme for measuring the quality of supply into a system of recognition, classification and categorization.

In successive stages, in addition to accommodation, it has incorporated restaurants, tour operators, travel agencies, events and professional unions within its system. It is currently working to define quality standards for occasional passenger carriage, golf courses, attractions and hiking trails.

TGCSA is the only officially recognized quality control body for tourism products, companies and destinations in South Africa. It is a self-financed public-private body composed of 19 agents representing 6,500 companies. Part of its success has been due to the support received from the country's tourism industry from the start and to the contributions provided by consumers.

The system is voluntary. Companies can choose the category and accredited external auditor who will verify conformity with the Council's criteria. The Council grants the recognition. Most of the auditors are autonomous. Establishments can rise to higher or fall to lower categories based on conformity, or lack thereof, with required standards. Other grounds for loss of category include the accumulation of complaints.

In consonance with the local reality and particularities, the attributes considered are fundamentally tangible and are based on conformity with minimum, generic or specific and mandatory requisites, including documentation and knowledge of the market and product. The company is evaluated annually for its services and facilities but is not penalized if some are found wanting. The final score based on the total points obtained during the evaluation determines the category.

Associated companies can use the Council's insignia in their communications and facilities, are listed in the only official guidebook and receive support from the South Africa Tourism promotion body, as well as communication campaigns targeting tourism intermediaries and final consumers. It is also an indispensable requisite for qualifying as a provider for government entities in the country.

There is a customer service and call centre that channels feedback as to services provided, but without neglecting other useful sources, including written feedback and the Internet.

3.2 Current practice of standardization in tourism

Many years have had to pass in order for there to appear to exist what we might call a "global awareness" about quality in tourism. After more than two decades of fragmented and uncoordinated national initiatives, and of models always stymied by the same difficulties, we may soon see the publication of the first international standards for hotels, active tourism and signposting.

For destinations standardization is much more complex. So many activities could be covered that the challenge is to maintain focus.

Standardization has been a controversial topic for the tourism sector, often rejected out of fear of repeating experiences with the inflexible, inconsistent and obsolete classification and categorization systems now in place. Tourism companies tend to regard standardization as detrimental to the added value of their own brands and differentiation, and as an additional regulatory burden.

While the interests of large tourism groups have influenced the posture of developed countries, emerging tourism destinations, with less know-how in this area, have looked to standardization to offset inadequate legal structures for the regulation and marketing of their incipient tourism supply.

The European Package Tour Regulations, while not a quality standard per se, are among the few examples of efforts to objectively define quality requirements, basic customer guarantees and provider responsibilities.

3.3 Is it feasible to certify a destination?

It is in fact technically possible to certify destinations. The scope of such certification would be a separate question.

From the point of view of quality (and its certification), understood as a voluntary option, a fundamental principle of the process should be to offer the same initial opportunities for all destinations. The bigger a destination, however, the more complicated the implementation, the more likely that quality gaps will be found and the more important it will be to achieve a harmonious level of quality.

Since the universe of providers is so disparate, it would be difficult to obtain a representative sample. If certification is to apply only to certain areas of a destination (those of greatest interest to tourists) the evaluation may omit some key providers. At many destinations, for example, the most representative hotels may not be located in the historic centre, which at emerging destinations may frequently undergo restoration works.

It would not be correct either to evaluate the quality of a destination based on the work of a destination management organization (DMO), which is not directly responsible for how companies function.

The certification of destinations therefore requires solid comparative criteria, permitting comparisons between destinations with the same characteristics, size and orientation.

Case study 3.3   **Destination quality standard (Colombia)**

Colombia has developed destination quality standards that concentrate on factors of environmental and social sustainability: NTS-TS 001-1, Tourism Destinations of Colombia: Sustainability Requisites; and NTS-TS 001-2, Beach Tourism Destinations. The sustainability requisites have been developed through a broad consensus-based process with the participation of more than 200 organizations – universities, professional associations, tourism promotion and planning entities, public departments, operators, consulting firms, restaurants and hotels.

Since their initial drafting in 2006, three destinations have been certified and another two are in the certification process, which attests to the complexity of working on a destination-wide scale.

The standards are to be included as part of the strategy of the Vice Ministry for Tourism to:

– Promote the use and development of quality technical processes and technologies applicable to the tourism sector;

– Improve the quality of tourism services and destinations in colombia;

– Facilitate access to markets; and

– Help consolidate colombia's position as a world-class tourism destination.

The project is being implemented with State assistance covering 80% of the cost.

The scope of application for the standards encompasses:

– The destination's geographic boundaries and its supply and infrastructure for inbound tourists, which need to be previously identified;

– The development of a documented procedure to identify, gain access to, and regularly evaluate compliance with laws applicable to the destination with respect to environmental, sociocultural and economic matters; and

– The existence of a management system to ensure sustainability in three areas: environmental, sociocultural and economic.

The standards stipulate that the system needs to accredit continuous activity with respect to:

– The division of responsibilities;

– The definition and execution of training, awareness and information activities; and

– Emergency prevention and response and the initiation of improvement activities.

The issues dealt with include:

– Protection of flora and fauna;

– Water and energy resource management;

– Management of environmental and sociocultural impact;

– Waste treatment;

– Use of chemical substances;

–   Measures to control pollution; and

–   Adoption of codes of conduct.

The standards also include requisites with respect to:

–   The promotion, management and conservation of cultural heritage;

–   Returns to the local community (colombia is a country of many indigenous, afro-colombian and raizal communities);

–   The prevention of sexual commerce, crime and begging;

–   The formalization of itinerant street trading;

–   The generation of basic statistics, including those to measure visitor satisfaction;

–   Job creation and the development of business capacity;

–   Security and control for tourism development, signposting; and

–   The interpretation of attractions and promotion of the destination.

The Quality Tourism Certificate is awarded only if 100% of the requisites have been met.

Part two
Quality implementation, management and tools

Chapter 4

Quality of a destination's environment

Summary   This chapter examines the elements that affect and shape the quality of a tourism destination.

Key words
- Value chain;
- Underlying factors; and
- Reputation.

Key message   The quality plans of a tourism destination need to strike a balance between the physical environment, the tourism value chain and what are called "underlying factors". Experience has shown such plans to be effective when designed and implemented on a local scale, which makes them useful as regional development instruments.

The destination, as perceived, *purchased* and judged by the tourist, is the premier tourism product. A kind of virtual enterprise, the destination is an interrelated system of providers that interact and form a chain of value, such that any performance failure by one provider affects all providers. The key to destination management is thus to deliver an appropriate, uniform and stable level of quality.

4.1   How to develop a quality plan for a destination

The success of any destination quality plan requires balance in considering three components of the tourism product which, though interconnected, need to be considered and attended to individually:
- The physical environment;
- The tourism value chain, which refers to the approach to be taken in delivering the services that go into the chain, often sequentially, and involve tourism, as well as other providers; and
- What are called "underlying factors" – physical, political and social environment; legal framework; business climate; accessibility; security – that form the context for competition and which are usually exogenous.

Quality can be implemented at four levels: supraregional, national, regional and local.

At the **supraregional level,** quality should be addressed by means of individualized work with the tourism subsectors (accommodation, operators, restaurants, etc.). While there have been international initiatives for quality tourism, no agreement has yet been reached on what different countries mean by quality or how to go about harmonizing regulations and interests.

Case study 4.1 **Central American Federation of Chambers of Tourism (FEDECATUR)**

In 1997, following a multilateral USAID project begun that year to strengthen their tourism sectors, the Central American Federation of Chambers of Tourism (FEDCATUR) decided to promote the programme SERVICE BEST, developed by the Alberta Tourism Education Council, and to acquire rights to use of its Quality License. Central American countries have shared a joint strategy and structure for promoting tourism ever since.

At the **national and regional levels** there have been several valuable experiences which, again, are based on individualized work with tourism subsectors although with the clear aim of moving toward an integrated approach. Systems have been designed to meet specific national needs in support of national promotion policies. Quality standards have been developed and independent entities established to monitor conformity with them and run the certification process. Notable examples of such efforts can be found in Spain, France, Switzerland, the United Kingdom, Germany, South Africa and China. China's effort has been unique in focusing solely on the outbound tourism market.

Such an approach to quality requires great financial capacity and tends to be viable for national institutions only – those concerned with quality, as well as those dedicated to tourism. Industry and other associations lead the process but require public economic support.

Case study 4.2 **Certification of quality services (China)**

With the aim of improving the quality of outbound tourism services, the China National Tourism Administration (CNTA) has implemented a Quality Certification Programme for Tourism Services, establishing certification and evaluation criteria for the local market.

The objectives of the programme are to:

- Promote cooperation among certified providers;
- Improve the quality of tourism services; and
- Stimulate and organize its incipient outbound market.

To date, 196 companies have joined the programme. The system is voluntary and intended for travel agencies, accommodation establishments, shops, tourist attractions and restaurants. Depending on each case analysis covers the following:

- Organizational aspects (years in operation, company profile, management team, capacity to contend with emergencies, absence of serious prior complaints, business hours, etc.);
- Resources and infrastructure, such as environment and surroundings, accessibility, facilities);
- Product requisites (such as design, menus, availability of information, signposting in Chinese, no imposed shopping time or visits to specific establishments during tours unless agreed to by the travellers);
- Processes (customer service, service consistency, payment facilities, reservations, tax refunds for purchases in the case of international travellers, sanitary conditions, etc.);
- Professional ethics (not resorting to dumping, contractual clarity, transparent policies about the changes and refunds, etc.); and
- Reputation (brand, comments by Chinese travellers).

Those interested in joining need to submit legal and other documentation, which may include photographs, a written commitment to quality, and a letter of recommendation from a relevant legal entity or association. The system offers assistance and checklists in connection with this process.

Beneficiaries can obtain certification and benefit from promotional activities organized by the CNTA.

At the **local level** (municipality, county, etc.) integration initiatives can be attempted: a shared vision of the destination's tourism sector, a limited number of relevant actors, a uniform image that also highlights distinguishing features, all facilitate the work and permits the destination quality plan to be oriented so as to address specific needs and make improvements that reduce the possibility of quality gaps. In this case, the system is more exposed to outside criticism and may be qualified as being made to *measure* if not supported technically. A quality system linked to broad-based external certification can strengthen credibility.

In all of the cases described, quality can be approached from two different perspectives at the same time: focusing on specific sectors but also in a crosscutting way on the destination as a whole, incorporating services *other* than tourism but related thereto: health, transport, infrastructure, commerce, banking, etc. This is the strategy being followed by Spain. Its advantage lies in a simultaneous approach to all aspects of quality in tourism, covering in particular:
–   Destinations (geographic scope);
–   The value chain; and
–   Underlying factors.

Its main disadvantage is the need for large financial investments and a longer timeframe for achieving substantial results.

Ultimately, how a destination performs in achieving quality cannot be separated from the supply offered by local tourism providers.

Theoretically, in a world where multilateral partnerships are increasingly needed, and are proliferating, it might be possible to combine all of the options. The path chosen will depend on the situation in each region, country or destination, as well as the competitive environment, reputation, level of development, acceptance of quality systems and awareness about them among operators predisposed to achieve quality.

4.1.1   The geographical dimension: destinations

Quality plans for destinations have different advantages depending on their scope.

Local plans may provide short-term results and can be much more precise in attending to the needs of local tourism industries and minimizing deficiencies in quality.

For destinations, unlike organizations or companies, the absence of leadership or policies committed to maintaining quality, making adjustments as necessary, can doom a plan to failure over time, for lack of supervision. In addition, the cost of implementing such a plan is proportionate to the destination's size and need for improvement.

Destination quality plans can serve as marketing and regional development instruments, as well as mechanisms for cohesion and product promotion, with the development of distinctive identifying elements (such as conformity marks or certification).

As in the case of plans for specific sectors, destination quality plans have the advantage of reducing the number of interlocutors, although the need to include the greatest number of actors possible may tend to undermine the requisites established for joining the system, something that needs to be corrected as the plan is consolidated.

4.1.2   Tourism value chain

Perceptions are important in considering strategies to achieve excellence in tourism.

Why do perceptions differ? The reasons are many and varied but it is basically because the tourism experience is captured in parts, and rarely as a whole. The hotel is experienced and judged separately from the airline, travel agency, bus, taxi, rental car, train, shop, restaurant, historic place, folkloric exhibition, convention centre and so on. Each of these *pieces* is not usually connected, in the visitor's mind, with the availability and quality of infrastructure (roads, airports, water, sewerage, communications, etc.), migration processes, security standards or food sanitation requirements. But all of these things affect the whole experience and need to be considered when a destination is evaluated.

Quality relates to the total experience. What is important for the tourist is the experience as a whole: the entire chain of experiences and the providers that form part of it.

The destination is the basic tourism product: tourists perceive, buy and value it as a whole. It is an inter-related system of providers interacting with the same clientele. The various actors engaged in tourism form a kind of virtual company and become partners in a value chain.

Figure 4.1   **Tourism value chain**

Source: Leo Partners consulting firm; adaptation.

A customer's level of satisfaction with a destination is based on the cumulative sum of his or her experiences in getting information, shopping, transit, accommodation or enjoyment. This sequence begins in the generating market. There is a mental process that does not distinguish components but rather focuses on the whole, such that any performance failure of one component affects the tourist's overall judgment of the whole.

The larger or more complex the destination, the more extensive its value chain and the greater likelihood of failures along the way. The key to managing the quality of a destination is maintaining an adequate, uniform and stable level of quality. There should be no important quality gaps between some providers and others nor between the different services engaged.

From that point of view, we can deduce that quality management in tourism destinations requires a comprehensive approach shared by producers and authorities alike. From that new perspective, quality should be understood as an integral part of an organization's tourism culture, professional ethic, management style, overall vision and modus operandi, taking a holistic approach to excellence.

Destinations should therefore consider controlling quality throughout the process, even for matters that are not their direct responsibility, such as the quality of information provided in tourism generating countries, by tourism intermediaries or by the press. A full-fledged destination quality system, structured according to the tourism value chain, will be based on:
–   The identification of possible differences between the quality expected by customers and the quality provided by each of the processes and services that make up the value chain;
–   Study and analysis of the causes of the deficiencies identified; and
–   The execution of remedial action plans.

In addition, when public and private actors work together to improve quality and solve particular problems, the challenges encountered can be turned to the destination's competitive advantage.

4.1.3   Underlying factors that influence a destination quality strategy

Destination quality strategies are influenced by diverse factors, as illustrated in the figure below.

Figure 4.2   **Underlying factors**

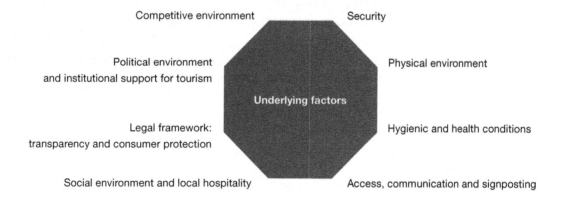

Security

The governments of many countries regularly review and classify the level of security of travel destinations and issue advisories to their citizens. Their assessment constitutes a prescriptive factor. Information is also regularly disseminated by the media and on the Internet about areas where travel is considered risky.

Risks can be linked to natural disasters, to social or political situations, or other potential disruptions to personal safety.

Negative information can be highly dissuasive. Apart from natural disasters and political conflicts, viruses such as bird flu A(H5N1) and Ebola, the eruption of the Eyjafjallajökull volcano, the tragically famous tsunamis in southeast Asia and Japan, the Arab Spring, armed conflict in Colombia, criminal gang violence in Mexico or even the garbage strike in Madrid have demonstrated the devastating power of negative information over tourist flows when a well-designed crisis management programme is not in place to counteract unfavourable media coverage for a destination.

One of the most dramatic cases in recent memory is that of a German family who after picking up their rental car upon arrival got lost and ended up in a part of Miami, Florida (United States of America) considered extremely dangerous. They were assaulted and one of the vehicle's occupants was killed. The story generated sharp reactions and severely impacted demand. The destination was required to wage an extensive communication campaign and car rental companies to provide tourists with detailed instructions and maps.

Communication during crises is a critical element of a good crisis management system. It helps to limit the negative impact of a crisis by meeting the information needs of all actors in the sector in an efficient, timely and responsible way. In this context, for the benefit of national tourism organizations (NTOs), destination management organizations (DMO's) and private sector entities working in the travel and tourism field UNWTO has developed complete and up-to-date *crisis communication tools for the tourism sector*.[1] These *tools* constitute a practical guide to contending effectively with the challenges posed by any crisis situation.

Destinations should be aware of how they are considered and evaluated in other countries with respect to security. Accordingly, they should make an effort to share information on positive initiatives to enhance security for tourists and develop an information containment and crisis management plan to help contend rapidly and efficiently with any negative publicity. The plan should target prescriptive opinion leaders, tourism intermediaries and final consumers.

In the same way, regulations, prevention plans and conduct protocols to reduce risks during travel need to be developed and disseminated to operators and tourists.

Physical environment

The forces of nature can turn the tourism industry upside down, disrupt travel and ultimately generate dissatisfaction. Increasingly unpredictable meteorological surprises, resulting from climate change, can be devastating for the sector – snowless winters at ski resorts or prolonged bad weather cutting the summer season short in coastal areas. Other phenomena, such as hurricanes, earthquakes, volcanic eruptions or tsunamis are less frequent and, up to a point, more predictable, thanks to technology. They remain, however, a real potential risk.

---

1   World Tourism Organization (2012), *Toolbox for Crisis Communications in Tourism – Checklists and best practices,* UNWTO, Madrid.

Hygienic and health conditions

Tourists can suffer accidents; bites and stings; disease; poisoning or infection; or parasites. Since security is an indispensable requisite, emphasis must be placed on preventing the causes of a danger or risk and knowing how to manage such situations.

Possible causes include the following:
– Inadequate sanitation and water and waste treatment;
– Imprudence or lack of precaution on the part of tourists, operators or authorities for visits to certain places (such as the jungle) or risky activities (such as rafting); and
– Inadequate food hygiene practices.

Managing their effects requires:
– Adequate information and signposting for visitors about possible risks at the destination or when visiting tourist attractions;
– Adequate human and technical resources; and
– Good coordination between authorities and tour operators.

There are destinations that lack even the most basic requisites for attending to accidents: antiophidic serum, cots, immobilization materials, adequate medical transport, etc. A destination cannot be developed if basic safety and health conditions, including guaranteed access to medical attention under normal circumstances, are deficient.

Any incident reflecting poor quality can have serious consequences for a destination's image once known to the market. A bad memory of a trip because of food poisoning or an accident not properly attended to can induce visitors not to return or recommend the destination.

Access, communication and signposting

The connectivity of destinations and accessibility to attractions depend, among other things, on the frequency, availability and duration of opportunities to visit them, as well as on signposting and adequate information before and during a stay or visit.

In today's interconnected world, facilitating access to communications is fundamental, and a matter of security. Internet access is the most appreciated hotel amenity.

Since an image is worth more than 1,000 words, the use of symbols easily recognizable by the tourist can help to bridge cultural or language differences. Their content, placement, arrangement and aesthetic character are attributes associated with quality.

Aware of their importance, UNWTO published a *Manual on Accessible Tourism for All: Public-Private Partnerships and Good Practices,*[2] the fruit of collaboration between UNWTO and the

2 World Tourism Organization and ACS Foundation (2014), *Manual de turismo accesible para todos – Alianzas público-privadas y buenas prácticas,* UNWTO, Madrid.

See also, in collaboration with ONCE Foundation and ENAT: World Tourism Organization (2014 and 2015), *Manual de Turismo Accesible para Todos – Principios, herramientas y buenas prácticas,* modules I–V, UNWTO, Madrid.

ACS Foundation to develop accessible heritage and cultural resources and facilitate the tactical knowledge necessary to make the built and natural environment accessible for tourist use as part of a public-private partnership strategy.

Social environment and local hospitality

The tourism vocation of a destination – the receptiveness and hospitality of the local population – is an essential part of the visitor's experience.

When tourism development does not take the interests of local communities or populations into account, it can generate hostility. It is essential to include the local population in the tourism process and find ways to raise their awareness, and empower and incentivize them, to reap the benefits of tourism activity.

Hostility can also be the result of a backlash effect, to the extent that the destination's success can create discomfort among residents as a result of the social, environmental and cultural pressure exerted by visitors.

Case study 4.3   **Strategic Plan for Tourism, Barcelona (Spain)**

Tourism growth in Barcelona has made the city a successful, internationally recognized destination. A multiplicity of elements makes it attractive to a wide range of demand segments, highly diverse in terms of origin and motivation. Most of the international classifications and studies place Barcelona among the best places and highlight visitor satisfaction, its values and qualities in terms of lifestyle, cultural supply and recreation, architectural and monumental legacy, hotel capacity, shopping and restaurants, as well as its vast supply of facilities for meetings industry tourism and conventions.

In terms of promotion, the work being done by *Turisme de Barcelona,* a public-private consortium composed of the Chamber of Commerce and the municipality, self-sufficient financially, is a much admired model. The results have been more than 10 million visitors, 25 million overnight stays and EUR 20 million daily in tourist spending.

The growth in tourism has been accompanied by criticisms from citizens about the problems derived from mass tourism and the rapid transformation of commercial activities that must coexist with tourism at tourist sites, which make it difficult for tourism to fit into city life. The failure to manage the negative impact of tourism clearly points to the need for a new tourism policy for the city. Prejudices and stereotypes surrounding tourists and tourism as being responsible for some of the city's problems presage the onset of tourism fatigue, which threatens the quality of life for citizens and ruins the experience for visitors.

The city's new Strategic Plan for Tourism is the fruit of a process of participation and shared reflection among citizens and institutions that establishes a roadmap for addressing challenges and a new model of tourism for the city, in an environment that is increasingly competitive, subject to economic crises and changing products and demand, while at the same time stemming the gentrification of this destination.

Legal framework: transparency and consumer protection

It should be recalled that tourism is not a product that can be examined in advance. Therefore, apart from verifying the professional and legal capacity of tourism providers and combating fraudulent activity, regulation of tourism must include and apply to the maximum extent the precepts of consumer protection in its broadest sense:

– Respecting the rule of law;
– Eliminating abusive contractual clauses and misleading wording;
– Guaranteeing the quality of products purchased; and
– Providing transparent information when packages and services are purchased or when prices are applied.

Political environment and institutional support for tourism

The development of quality at a tourism destination requires a proper framework for institutional collaboration.

National tourism organizations (NTOs) are responsible for putting tourism policies into practice, including promotion and representation abroad. Their competences include planning, product development, market research, promotional marketing and event financing or management, among others. They are responsible for overseeing provider qualifications and quality by means of licensing and classification systems. Their local counterpart for particular destinations is the destination management organization (DMO), increasingly of public-private composition.

Their work generates expectations among potential customers through promotion and concrete initiatives to structure and regulate the market, for example through brands and the categorization of products.

Compiling and interpreting tourism statistics and conducting market research can help the industry by profiling market segments and identifying trends in demand, patterns of behaviour and visitor expectations and perceptions, so as to plan promotional efforts accordingly. The reliability, updating and accessibility of such statistics are key issues in the quality process, helping to pinpoint needs and develop products to meet them.

Given the crosscutting character of tourism, it is also important to attend to other needs, such as:
– Imports and exports of goods, in the case of handicrafts;
– The condition of communication infrastructure or signposting at tourist transit points;
– Personnel training and qualification;
– Attraction of investments; and
– The treatment of taxes generated by tourism; and
– Management of heritage or the circulation of capital.

These aspects are the responsibility of such disparate departments of public administration as finance, transport, environment, labour, culture, economic affairs and external affairs.

Competitive environment

In a global market, destinations compete against each other. But a competitor need not necessarily be a nearby destination. The variables of competition may arise from different factors:
– *Location* (the Caribbean and equivalent products compete against each other);
– *Specialization* (Peru, Mexico, Guatemala, Egypt, Italy, Turkey and Thailand compete in the archaeological tourism segment); and

–   *Size* (in the case of receiving markets, such as Spain, France, Italy or the United States of America, or cities whose tourism figures are comparable to those in many countries, including the major European and North American capitals).

So competition takes place at different levels. Outlining a map of competition entails among other things:
–   Comparing prices, quality, strategies and results;
–   Identifying aspects that distinguish a destination; and
–   Identifying what measures must be taken to strengthen and protect a destination's unique character.

4.2   Destination image and reputation

Would our conception of a quality tourism destination include one where tourism providers as such provide high quality services but where the airport, for example, is falling apart, supplies and public services are not scaled to accommodate the population influx during high season, the sanitation system malfunctions, shopping possibilities are inadequate, health care services are insufficient or social conflict has erupted?

By virtue of its crosscutting character as an economic activity, tourism and the final image of a destination depend on actors, services and entities that may not at first glance seem tourism-related, and in respect of which tourism authorities have no role to play: banking, commerce, police, public transport, etc.

Communication activities, the performance of institutions, together with components of the value chain, physical environment and so-called underlying factors, also help to shape a destination's image. Some are common, such as security. But others depend on the type of destination. Mobility and the availability of parking, for example, is a critical factor for the image of large cities, whereas in the case of heritage destinations, tourists tend to be more sanguine about it.

How a destination is managed, combined with value judgments, perceptions, opinions and recommendations freely expressed by citizens and visitors, shape the destination's reputation. Reputation, in turn, generates trust, attraction, patronage.

Reputation is an ethical, strategic and transformational concept for a destination that involves everyone and that is nourished by facts and actions. Not marketing promises, which is what distinguishes reputation from the concept of a brand, whose purpose is fundamentally transactional. While the ability of public entities to affect a destination's reputation is limited, their role in assuring quality is quite important. According to econometric models developed by the Reputation Institute,[3] a single point improvement in reputation can produce a 50% increase in tourism income for some destinations, as a function of their attractiveness and the inclination of travellers to spend money there. On the other hand, loss of reputation can have catastrophic economic consequences.

---

3   Estudio City RepTrak®: http://reputationinstitute.es/thought-leadership/category/city-reptrak (25-05-2015).

Chapter 5

Implementation of quality at destination level

Summary This chapter describes the elements that should go into a quality plan, its territorial scope, key aspects that define an excellent destination, and the roadmap, time and investments required to implement it at the destination. A reference model, the European Foundation for Quality Management (EFQM), is also included.

Key words
- Quality system;
- Quality committee;
- EFQM;
- Dashboard;
- Total quality; and
- Destination management organization (DMO).

Key message Implementing a quality plan means developing a quality system as a mechanism for making substantial improvements and maintaining them over time.

The development of a destination plan is a project involving four phases and requiring at least two years of work to obtain relevant results, depending on such factors as resource availability, actor awareness and commitment, and implementation strategy. The current tendency is toward self-regulation with private sector participation, since the keys to success are conviction, commitment (financial and other) and the participation of destination actors.

5.1   How to implement a destination quality system?

5.1.1   What is a quality system?

When we talk about a quality plan we actually refer to a system of quality assurance ("quality system" for short). Implicit in any quality plan should be the development of a quality system. A quality system is a management mechanism that permits substantial improvements to be made and maintained over time.

There is no place in our concept of quality for cosmetic, ad hoc measures: when companies, entities or destinations allow inertia to take over they fall again and again into the same errors. A quality system is an endless process, with short-, medium- and long-term milestones but continuing indefinitely.

The term quality management system or quality assurance system refers to a company's or destination's activities, procedures, processes and resources, with a view to instilling and managing quality. It defines the *how,* not the *what.*

Such systems incorporate a range of integrated technical and administrative activities, which include planning, implementation, evaluation, information and quality improvement, to ensure that a process, product or service meets customer expectations. If the organization is not properly controlled and conditions and measures are not established to make quality a habit, it will be difficult to ensure consistency in the products and services offered.

Every quality system depends on real commitment from the actors concerned, lacking which, three-quarters of all quality plans fail.

This commitment has to materialize in the identification of priorities, systematic monitoring, the establishment of communication channels, the formulation of policies, funding, and the settlement of any disputes that may arise.

Case study 5.1   **Tourism quality system (Dominican Republic)**

The Dominican Republic is developing a Comprehensive Quality System based on technical standards for eight tourism-related sectors (transport, restaurants, accommodation, inbound agencies, shops, artisans, guides and museums, and visitable centres), which includes the development of a brand or seal and instruments to support implementation, including a guide, checklist and audit mechanism.

5.1.2   The quality committee

The cornerstone for implementing a quality plan or system is a quality committee, composed of destination leaders and institutions. Its functions include:
- Promoting a culture of quality;
- Defining a quality policy and its objectives;
- Developing procedures;
- Managing and supervising the quality system;
- Managing documentation; and
- Gathering and analysing records to evaluate performance, proposing and executing corrective action and continuous improvement plans.

Varying in composition with respect to number and form, the quality committee is comparable to a destination management organization (DMO), irrespective of who takes part, their legal personality or title.

It is advisable for quality committees to hold regular meetings and hire a qualified expert on quality control, at least part-time or through external contract.

5.1.3   Roadmap for implementing a destination quality plan

A destination quality plan consists of four phases:
1.   Evaluation or diagnostic assessment;
2.   Design;
3.   Implementation; and
4.   Control.

The diagnostic assessment, design and implementation take at least one year of work and depend on several factors: the availability of resources, the awareness and commitment of relevant actors in respect of quality, the implementation strategy (mandatory or voluntary), etc. To achieve significant results takes another year of operation.

It is probable that during the process destination actors will criticize each phase of the plan and the time allocated for it, which they may consider insufficient to achieve mass participation and consensus. Experience has shown, however, that slowing down each phase can be interpreted as a sign of inefficiency, dwindling interest and an open door to the relaxation of standards.

Evaluation

The objective of this phase is to assess the baseline situation with respect to the destination's quality strengths and weaknesses. No one ever starts from zero.

The process needs to determine the attributes that visitors consider relevant and to what extent, identifying customer needs and expectations on the one hand (demand) and those of local destination companies, institutions and authorities on the other (supply). Comparing the results for each could expose and explain quality gaps between the supply and demand sides.

In developing subsequent activities, either to improve quality or introduce a quality system, emphasis will be placed on reducing the gaps considered to be of highest priority, in terms of the room for improvement identified or the impact it might have on consumer choices.

A destination's residents and intermediaries, in their capacity as prescriptive opinion leaders, represent another potential target for evaluation. Lastly, though not indispensable, it may be useful to learn the viewpoint of qualified observers (consisting essentially of experts, academics, opinion leaders and specialized journalists), to round out the picture.

A battery of tools is available to help analyse the information, as described in chapter 9.

Design

There are different options for developing a destination quality plan depending on the scope, approach and attributes concerned:

1. Scope	2. Approach	3. Attributes
– The product; and – The destination management system.	– Sectoral; – Cross-cutting; and – Mixed.	– Tangible elements; and – Intangible elements.

- **Scope:** there are two options:
    1. Product improvement through specific, limited and temporary measures; this is the easiest and fastest option with results to be expected over the short term; or
    2. The establishment of a destination quality assurance system.
    Since the first will presumably represent an as-needed, case-by-case option, we will focus on the second, the only capable of permitting significant, lasting improvements. If that is the aim, the second option is indeed the more advisable, since the first requires constant updating and does not cover the destination as a whole, or resolve structural problems. The first is linked to a parallel certification mechanism, the second is not.

Improvements introduced through a quality destination system will be reflected in the coordination, management, promotion, and economic and social benefits – as well as in the products and innovative capacity – of tourism activity.

– **Approach:** at the level of the destination we can also consider whether to focus on specific subsectors, take a more comprehensive, crosscutting approach, or do both, which is undoubtedly the most advisable alternative. The Quality Tourism Plan developed by Spain, the world's first such initiative, focused first on the subsectors – hotels in particular – with a view to obtaining a demonstration effect for other subsectors and destinations.

Today, with the experience we now have, narrowing a destination's initial focus to specific subsectors would be justifiable only from a financial standpoint.

– **Attributes:** as our final set of options we can focus the plan solely on tangible attributes or on tangible, as well as intangible ones. The first option is more advisable for emerging destinations that need to organize and guarantee basic aspects of their hotels, restaurants or attractions, or in other words destinations without sufficient capacity, resources or experience in these areas. As intangible attributes are incorporated into the plan, the destination's distinguishing features and competitive market position can be strengthened.

It is advisable to include a benchmarking process during this phase, to learn from the experience of other destinations that have implemented quality plans, particularly with regard to ways of overcoming implementation barriers, the attributes and indicators selected and the strategies applied to reducing identified quality gaps.

The plan need not be very sophisticated: simplicity redounds in favour of wider and faster implementation. It is very important, on the other hand, to have a sound technical basis for the points of reference used in designing the quality plan or system, so as to give assurances of reliability to the market and potential participants.

Chapter 6 provides a detailed explanation of the process of designing the system, a toolkit for supporting the process, the definition of standards, the assignment of responsibilities and development of procedures, all essential parts of this phase.

Implementation

The implementation process is based on four main elements:

1. The participation and commitment of destination actors, to be achieved through an **awareness** raising effort. Workshops are conducted to explain the scope, expected benefits, commitments entailed, tools and functioning of the system, including any recognition awarded as incentives to motivate participants.

2. **Training and technical assistance:** designation of a quality specialist to coordinate implementation and advise companies and participating entities. Possibilities for outsourcing of the advisory assistance and training by expert consultants should not be dismissed. Implementation guides, self-evaluation handbooks and documentary examples of the quality system can facilitate the involvement of organizations and companies. A simple drafting style that is accessible and avoids technical language facilitates understanding of the concepts and the work to be done.

3. Development of a detailed **improvement plan** according to the gaps detected, with the participation of all destination actors; and

4. **Identification of quality indicators** for use in measuring the current situation, making adjustments to the improvement plan and establishing future objectives.

Control

Procedures are applied to the results of business processes to generate records (complaints, analysis of indicators, internal audits, surveys, etc.) to measure the effectiveness of the system put in place and any updating required. In a changing global marketplace monitoring results is crucial.

5.1.4 Models of excellence

Existing models should be used to promote quality on a destination-wide scale. Experience in that regard has been limited and fragmentary.

We can speak of *total quality* when models surpass minimum standards and self-improvement efforts are unwavering. Total quality models can be applied to destinations, but their principles need to be interpreted.

They all share some common characteristics:
- A focus on customer satisfaction;
- Managerial leadership (in the case of a destination a technocratic structure composed of local government, institutions and local leaders) as the only way to ensure consistency between strategy and corporate culture;
- Planning based on the principle of continuous improvement, i.e. Measuring effectiveness, monitoring, setting challenges or improving results over time;
- Defined working procedures and standards to ensure consistency of products and services;
- Effective management;
- A system of fluid communication among customers, employees and management, as a source of strategic information for improvement; and
- The mobilization and commitment of all concerned parties to achieving the established goals.

5.1.5 Applicability of the EFQM Model to destinations

The most advanced model for total quality is the European Foundation for Quality Management (EFQM).

It is divided into two distinct, equally important sections, which are subdivided into a total of nine criteria: a first group of five concerning "agents or facilitators" – i.e. the mechanisms for managing the organization – and an equally important and corresponding second group of four concerning "results". The results are indicative of success in managing the enterprise and the actors concerned determine how to achieve them.

Each of the nine weighted criteria comprises a series of sub-criteria and, in turn, each of these provides a list of areas for analysis, which are neither exhaustive nor compulsory. The criteria and their weights are as follows:
- Leadership (10%);
- People (9%);
- Policy and strategy (8%);

- Partnerships and resources (9%);
- Processes (14%);
- Results (people) (9%);
- Results (customers) (20%);
- Results (society) (6%); and
- Key business results (15%).

Although EFQM was created to help achieve improvements using universal criteria, its application to each particular destination has proven more complicated, requiring adaptation for such factors as the multiplicity of organizations belonging to different sub-sectors, the volume and disparity of information generated and pending analysis or the breadth of applicable indicators.

Figure 5.1   **Quality model: European Foundation for Quality Management (EFQM)**

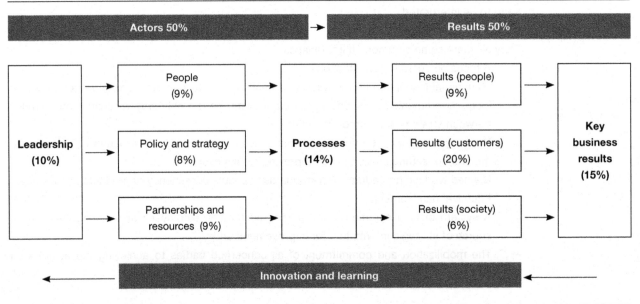

One possible interpretation of the nine criteria, already applied by a number of pilot projects, is the following:

Leadership

The concept of leadership covers the aims and values of quality and the conduct of the destination's institutional leaders in respect of total quality.

This quality function can be labelled "organization and management". It refers to the work of public administrations, as well as various forms of public-private partnership, some very effective.

In all destinations defined as such there should be a supervisory entity capable of structuring the tourism planning process, the product, its promotion and image, and establishing mechanisms for public-private and inter-administrative collaboration, however it might be labelled. The application of the EFQM model to a destination attaches great importance to such bodies, as being responsible for leading the process.

Assuming leadership necessarily means taking a proactive, catalysing position, acting as reference, raising awareness among actors, encouraging the introduction of good practices and quality systems and assisting organizations forming part of the destination's supply, providing resources in that connection if necessary.

Policy and strategy

This criterion is based on the destination's final objectives, how they can be achieved and how the supervisory body brings the values of quality to the destination. It is embodied in plans, actions, processes and communication, the identification of tourist needs and opportunities for improvement, with mechanisms for actor participation, opportunities for self-assessment and benchmarking with similar destinations.

People

At all destinations there are key actors – institutions, companies or market leaders – whose behaviour marks a tendency.

The managing authority is responsible for developing and improving the destination's competitive posture, drawing from local skills and knowledge and from the valuable experience and information maintained by frontier personnel for use in improving the destination; promoting effective communication; and recognizing the efforts of its personnel.

Being a high quality tourism destination means implementing a culture of quality and hospitality, encouraging teamwork among actors, and involving people in the duties and responsibilities entailed.

Partnerships and resources

The model applies criteria for:
– Zoning, management, strengthening, rational use and preservation of the destination's facilities, infrastructure, heritage and business resources;
– Their adaptation for purposes of tourism (signposting, restaurants, information, accessibility, receptive capacity); or
– The application to businesses of quality and environmental management systems.

It also includes the criteria for detecting opportunities and possible partnerships to create value and synergies, as well as mechanisms for the exchange of knowledge.

Tourism destinations with similar dynamics frequently need to generate synergies through policies of partnership and collaborative networks, and even to share the same brand, as in the case of UNESCO heritage destinations, slow cities, etc.

Process

> This refers to the management of activities that contribute value added to the destination's supply. In contrast with the model prevailing between 1970 and 1980, when operators played a preponderant role in the marketing and design of tourism products, destinations today take direct responsibility for satisfying the desires of demand, how their products are perceived and what their supply consists of.

> Quality, in terms of visitor satisfaction, is the fruit of a chain of processes or activities. Destinations often react late to changing demand trends and do not generally analyse the causes.

Results for employees

> Quality can also be assessed in terms of employee satisfaction, as measured by means of workplace, business climate and market studies, to establish the extent to which quality in this area supports the destination's competitiveness.

Results for customers (visitors to the destination)

> Level of satisfaction with respect to the destination is assessed by means of surveys or similar methods, which elicit perceptions about services, motivation or likelihood of recommending the destination.

Results for society

> Tourism development is justified only to the extent that it produces balanced benefits for the visitor and local society.

> The criterion "results for society" pertains to the more profound objectives, directly associated with the concept of sustainability, that tourism should seek to advance.

> In most places where they have been introduced, destination quality plans have brought benefits, first of all, for the local population, bringing solutions to issues that tourism has pushed to the forefront or that have reached a scale permitting or justifying greater public investment in the improvement of services and infrastructure. In the mountains of Navarra, in Spain, for example, a destination quality plan enabled a cluster of small municipalities dispersed in four valleys to identify a quality gap affecting visitors and residents alike: a lack of coordination in terms of geographic location and working hours between medical emergency facilities and on-duty pharmacies.

Key results for tourism destinations

> This criterion summarizes and analyses the progress made by a tourism destination as a result of the quality initiatives undertaken, whether specific to each subsector or generic for the destination as a whole.

The achievements of the destination are collected, sorted and analysed using a system of indicators based on:

- Key business results (in terms of productivity, occupancy, average expenditure, etc.);
- The various socio-economic indicators;
- Customer satisfaction complaints and suggestions; and
- Comparative analysis, if possible, with similar destinations.

The adoption of consensus-based strategies is directly related to the income of the activity, and as such, any effort must be measured and analysed in light of the results.

Case study 5.2   **Comprehensive Destination Quality Model (SICTED) (Spain)**

Since 2000 Spain has been a pioneer in the development of a specific, experimental application of EFQM to destinations: the Comprehensive Destination Quality Model *(SICTED – Sistema Integral de Calidad Turística en Destinos),* a project to improve the quality of tourism destinations promoted by Spain's Ministry of Tourism (Secretaría de Estado de Turismo) and the Spanish Federation of Municipalities and Provinces *(Federación Española de Municipios y Provincias – FEMP),* with the ultimate objective of improving the tourist's experience and satisfaction at destinations in the country.

SICTED is characterized by a single common methodology and as many different applications as there are types of destination. It provides a methodology for diagnostic assessment, a permanent, integrated system of quality management for tourism destinations based on a new conception of expected results, an emphasis on continuous improvement and an attitude predisposed toward recovery and enhancement of local resources. It is a feedback-based planning model designed around a comprehensive understanding of the destination and the identification of common objectives for the actors involved. It is implemented on the basis of annual cycles.

SICTED pursues a homogeneous level of quality in the services offered by a destination to tourists so that they do not perceive substantial differences between the different products offered by its various actors who make up the destination's supply, which would have a negative effect on tourist perceptions and satisfaction.

Among other tools it offers 32 good practice handbooks, one for each link in the value chain (hotels, travel agencies, transport, restaurants, etc.), as well as tangentially related services (public transport, commerce, etc.). Some of these subsectors are unique to a particular territory: cider bars, wineries, flamenco clubs.

SICTED offers member tourism companies/services a training plan, technical assistance by qualified advisors, group workshops and evaluations as to the company/service's conformity with quality standards. The process culminates in bestowal of the Tourism Quality Commitment award as recognition for the effort and commitment that distinguishes the establishment from its competition. The award is valid for two years, subject to a follow-up annual evaluation.

SICTED thereby serves two purposes:

1.   Operationally, it promotes and improves the quality of individual companies; and

2.   Strategically, it gathers, measures and analyses the quality indicators of tourism destinations and other key information as a basis for action to solidify their present and future competitive positioning.

SICTED has three important elements that distinguish it from traditional models:

1.   A battery of indicators, some voluntary others mandatory, some common to all destinations and others related to a destination's specialized character (rural, coastal, urban, heritage, etc.) with the aim of facilitating benchmarking. There is also a third group specific to each destination. It is a feedback-based, technologically-driven system. The definition of indicators has facilitated consensus among different public departments and authorities with tourism-related responsibilities about the destination's needs and the measures to be taken in consequence;

2.   An awareness and feedback component for destination actors and components of supply, since their direct exposure to tourists makes them a preferred target for SICTED and the main support for all strategic actions at a destination, aimed at collecting, integrating, prioritizing, complementing and rationalizing the needs expressed by the tourism industry and its customers; and

3.   The resulting destination management organization (DMO), regardless of the other functions it might acquire according to the characteristics of each specific destination, is a driving force for quality, offering assistance to all local partners, whether or not they are specifically part of the tourism industry.

The introduction of DMOs is the essential technical solution contributed by SICTED. The DMO is a permanent public-private structure concerned with developing a destination's tourism-related public services and the competitiveness of local companies. It has the capacity to manage the destination collectively for the benefit of all actors (including residents), which requires it to be based on participation, shared responsibility, collaboration and consensus.

DMO composition varies according to the destination concerned. In some cases DMO's have taken on the legal structure not of an association but of a company. They are generally made up of hoteliers, tour operators, public authorities (concerned with the environment, health, security, public works), merchants and even the clergy and/or army (as owners and administrators of many tourist attractions). DMO's have managers responsible for coordinating the action taken at the destination.

The model has been conducive for most DMO's to transitioning toward financial autonomy, though this is not always possible, depending on the characteristics of each destination.

DMO's are coordinated nationally by the Inter-Destination Committee, a participatory body established for the exchange of information about activities and changes being effected through the introduction of SICTED by participating destinations; the harmonization of activities carried out by each of the destinations; and supervision of the model's proper implementation. The committee is composed of representatives of Tourspain (Turespaña), FEMP, the Autonomous Communities, the Provincial Councils and destinations.

This makes the DMO a strategic figure in a destination's planning and structuring. The result has been better coordination and commitment among local actors. Companies that join the system voluntarily can participate in forums for improvements and help generate the information needed to manage the destination.

It has also been demonstrated that the implementation of good practices can be a more rapid, efficient and appropriate way to implement quality in SMEs, making it accessible for companies that for reasons of cost, resources, size or strategy would find it difficult to conform to existing quality standards and certification requirements. The great majority gained public recognition for their commitment to quality.

A destination's dashboard is an indispensable tool for the management of continuous improvement through measurement and analysis of the destination's current and projected conditions. Consisting of a battery of selected indicators its purpose is to reflect the collective quality of the destination, how it may be changing over time, and how its performance measures up to visitor expectations.

Both the EFQM Excellence Model and SICTED follow the P-D-C-A (Plan–Do–Check–Act) cycle methodology, in which the objectives to be achieved and activities to be developed are based on the results obtained, which are evaluated using a variety of indicators.

While the EFQM Model gives great importance to facilitating agents, SICTED focuses on results by evaluating the destinations dashboard of indicators. So there is a difference in the treatment of the criteria, though not of substance.

Similarly, SICTED does not separately examine the four results criteria of the EFQM model but sorts the indicators according to subsector, cross-sector standards and "global indices of destination quality".

The EFQM model features indicators not included in the SICTED model, which is based on rigorous selection to ensure operability and avoid "paralysis by analysis", (attending to all of the multi-sector and multifunctional complexity of a tourism space or destination). The destination's dashboard is merely a transposition of the criteria envisaged as key results of the tourism destination.

SICTED has been consolidated as a basic tool for destination management and the public decision processes of authorities in Spain. Its participants include 110 destinations and 6,500 companies, 3,000 of which have earned awards, making this a model for reference world-wide.

5.2   The role of public authorities in driving quality

Few economic sectors operate so globally, as well as regionally and locally – and yet are so subject to public intervention – as tourism, in which governments participate openly as market actors.

Governments do have a role to play as leaders and catalysts, which requires both a long-term strategic vision and the ability to react to market changes. This explains the search for new organizational forms capable of gathering the support and participation of local destination actors. The modern management entities being put in place are involved not just in promotion but in planning, product creation and destination management as a collective good.

5.2.1   Who should participate in tourism standardization?

Relegating participation in standard-setting processes to the private sector has led to the early death of many quality initiatives, for lack of private sector support.

A reasonable mechanism for promoting the implementation of quality is to link incentives, promotions or official contracts with adherence to quality plans.

When the standardization process does not consider the opinions of tourist consumers or market studies analysing their needs, the standards developed (which may pertain to hallway width, square meters available per person or minimum diameter of plates) do not reflect consumer interest or demand or the unique character of companies or destinations.

Implementing quality requires conviction and participation. Many quality plans lacking these ingredients have lost momentum. Similarly, a lack of destination-wide consensus has led to failure in the implementation of quality and reduced it to unrepresentative areas of focus once the motivating environmental factors, pressure from administrations or presence of consultants has disappeared.

Public-private cooperation is therefore necessary: in addition to fulfilling their commitments to a destination's quality, authorities need to play a facilitating, structuring and financing role as well (at least during start-up).

5.2.2   Should a scheme be mandatory or voluntary?

Although voluntary involvement is a fundamental principle of quality, authorities often push for mandatory processes, convinced that this will drive widespread implementation in the short term and facilitate promotion in the market.

The fact that some regulations need inherently to be mandatory (security, health, food hygiene) does not justify the implementation of mandatory schemes for hotel categorization or quality drafted behind the hotel sector's back. Used as an administrative tool such schemes have proven ineffective and rigid in the face of constantly changing demand, aside from creating an attitude of rejection within the industry.

Instead of the pursuit of excellence and continuous improvement, a mandatory approach is disorienting when trying to determine what competitive deficiencies the plan should target and even lead to rejection by participating businesses and a tendency to get by with the minimum compliance required.

The current trend is toward self-regulation. This does not mean that the initiative should be left exclusively in private-sector hands but that the sector should be involved in all phases of the plan, particularly the design phase.

5.2.3   Financing a quality plan

Development cost depends on the country concerned, the size of the destination, the scope of the plan and the availability of local expertise and experience in both quality and tourism. Although it is not strictly necessary, a large investment in promotion and communication, which can easily triple the design and implementation costs, is nonetheless justified, since the development of recognition mechanisms is an incentive for adherence to the plan and a tool for promotional marketing of the destination.

Quality plans are usually formalized in several waves, like concentric circles, expanding in scope and number of participants. Attempting from the start to tackle the entire destination in all its complexity can prove a pipe dream.

Once the first wave has been completed, with the plan fully in operation and a critical mass of actors involved and working on quality, it is advisable for public administrations to gradually reduce their economic contribution in favour of public-private co-financing models. Requiring an economic contribution from participating actors, even if merely nominal, will reduce the number of adherents but increase their commitment.

5.2.4   Structural models of public-private cooperation

Destinations have tourism structures at three sublevels, whose scope of action varies from country to country:
1.   Regional structures (governments, communities or states);
2.   County structures (multiregional demarcation); and
3.   Local/city structures.

These three levels combine to form six types of *multi-actor* bodies.[1]

In terms of models for inter-organizational collaboration, financial contributions need to be distinguished from physical participation. In some countries, governments do not have representatives in the organizations but public capital remains essential to the sector (according to UNWTO, 60% of the budgets of these tourism organizations depend on public funds). This

---

1   Zapata, M. J. and Hall, M. (2012), 'Public-private collaboration in the tourism sector: balancing legitimacy and effectiveness in local tourism partnership', *Journal of Policy Reseach in Tourism, Leisure Tond Events*, volume 4 (1), Routledge (online), available at: http://dx.doi.org/10.1080/19407963.2011.634069 (25-05-2015).

is for several reasons: the extreme fragmentation of the tourism industry; its weak operational capacity, representativeness and professionalism; the lack of critical mass in emerging or rural locations and a consequent lack of resources.

Some destinations have adopted public-private cooperation mechanisms such as the semi-public enterprises known as destination management organizations (DMOs).

In the development of these management organizations, local governments and entrepreneurs have played a growing and increasingly dynamic role. They have tended to evolve into independent organizational structures, such as convention bureaus and tourism consortia, among others. In many cases, however, public representatives maintain their leadership and private participation is often more testimonial than effective.

The semi-public management model does not in principle appear to be the most advisable way, at least at the start, for destinations to drive quality improvements.

Case study 5.3   **National Quality Plan (Spain)**

The Spanish National Quality Plan was the first to be developed by a public authority or destination and has reached an interesting critical mass. The development of a common methodology has led to the establishment of reciprocal guarantees across sub-sectors and destinations. Pioneering and well documented, it has been systematically used as an international reference model.

It was a response to a loss of competitiveness in Spanish tourism in the early 1990s, which caused a 28% decline in overall tourism revenues.

Following a pilot effort for hotels and holiday apartments in Puerto de la Cruz (Canary Islands), in 1995, Spain's General Secretariat of Tourism, in 1996, launched the Futures Plan, focusing on the recovery of tourism destinations and based on improving quality as a differentiating factor. This was followed by a Comprehensive Quality Plan for Spanish Tourism *(PICTE – Plan Integral de Calidad del Turismo Español)*.

From a promotional standpoint, it was argued that quality would reduce the inevitable pressure on prices. The Futures Plan laid the grounds for the subsequent development of the Spanish Tourism Quality System, with different but complementary areas of focus, which include:

- *Product quality,* adapting supply to new needs on the demand side, as a means of diversifying and mitigating seasonality. Networks and so called "Product Clubs" were introduced to facilitate joint product development and promotion at national and supraregional levels. They focus on and help to shape differentiating, special product characteristics as the basis for company affiliation. Examples include the Camino de Santiago, the Via de la Plata Route, Wine Routes of Spain, Fishing Villages, Thermal Villas, Jewish Quarters Network, the Don Quijote Route and the World Heritage Cities Club;

- *Training in quality assurance;*

- *Quality in sectors,* which results from a standardization effort through business self-regulation, technical and economic support for the implementation of voluntary quality systems in enterprises (compatible with existing categorization), establishment of the Institute for Spanish Tourism Quality *(ICTE – Instituto para la Calidad Turística Española)* and the promotion of a single brand. Nearly 2,000 enterprises in all sectors are registered in the system;

  The Service Quality Standards are minimal standards in terms of results (product or service delivery) for different services, as well as those related to systems and methods (processes) necessary to ensure the quality of services, defined on the basis of visitor aspirations and specifically for each of the tourism sectors (hotels, rural houses, travel agencies, tourist information offices, etc.). These standards represent a midpoint between ISO 9000 and EFQM; and

- *Quality at destinations,* which is based on sustainability, the commitment of residents and companies, as well as the leadership of local administrations and key local actors, through integrated management mechanisms, the regeneration of mature destinations and development of the potential of emerging destinations.

In 1998, the Green Municipality project was launched. It was designed to facilitate the adoption of environmental management criteria at tourism destinations with reference to ISO standard 14000. The project was initially hampered by a lack of specific resources and technical preparation for local administrations, which delayed the implementation.

With three-year budgets equally co-financed by State, autonomous and local administrations, the plans of excellence or dynamism helped to reposition and improve mature destinations or increase their awareness as destinations, structure their products and acquire management, development and promotion skills.

The need to integrate all of these efforts (at the sector and destination levels) became clear starting in 2000, with the launching of the Comprehensive Destination Quality Model (SICTED):

– *Quality and innovation:* research, promotion of new technologies and the development of applications, information, transaction, and reservation systems; and

– *Promotion of quality:* transformation of ICTE standards into UNE[a] standards, creation of a model and reference framework by means of international cooperation agreements and technology transfer, promotion and internationalization of the Q Mark and active participation in working groups of the international standardization bodies, including the European Normalization Committee (CEN) and the International Standardization Organization (ISO).

---

a)   UNE *(Una Norma Española,* or "A Spanish Standard") is a set of technological standards created by the Technical Standardization Committees which bring together all of the entities and actors concerned with and interested in each committee's work, as a general rule: AENOR (see note on page 125 – List of acronyms and abbreviations), manufacturers, consumers and users, governments, laboratories and research centres. Following their creation they undergo a trial period and are revised as necessary. The process is similar in other countries.

Chapter 6

Quality management

Summary   This chapter reviews the elements that go into a quality system and a few basic related concepts.

Key words
- Quality policy;
- Quality costs;
- Process;
- Procedure;
- Attribute;
- Indicator; and
- Standard.

Key message   The quality of a destination is more than the sum of its parts. It cannot be correctly evaluated solely on the basis of supply; visitors' opinions must also enter into consideration.

When a quality system is implemented it is best to work on a limited, selective and consensus-based number of objectives, which need to be communicated to the market and throughout the destination.

The implementation of a quality system requires documentary support, outlining the approach taken and the objectives pursued, common key procedures and records that reflect the implementation and results. Managing the quality system means measuring its effectiveness at regular intervals with respect to reference points, standards or objectives defined by the destination itself.

The quality of a destination is defined according to various service attributes – physical, intangible, as well as organizational and attitudinal – of importance to customers. Standards, on the other hand, refer to an objective level of quality that the destination aspires to achieve. To control the processes over time and evaluate the effectiveness and timeliness of improvements, we use measurable indicators representative of the attributes.

The process is managed by a Quality Committee, comparable to a DMO, with varying composition in terms of numbers and form.

Many organizations approach the question of quality without conviction, often assuming that a certain percentage of failures is inevitable and a cost of doing business. But it turns out that quality is profitable, capable of improving returns by up to 35%.

6.1   Diagnostic assessment of the quality of a destination

The quality of a destination is more than the sum of its individual components (hotels, restaurants, hospitality, transport, museums, etc.). There are crosscutting issues, such as cleanliness, security or authenticity, among others, that customers experience in terms of the entire destination. A good portion of such components are delivered by providers and institutions apparently unrelated to tourism: the police, banking, municipal services, commerce, etc.

It is a mistake to evaluate the quality of a destination exclusively from a supply perspective. A destination's quality is not a matter of higher class hotels or a high percentage of certified companies; unlike the quality of a company, a destination's quality does not result from mandatory compliance with minimum levels. It is a matter of achieving maximums. Only a comparison between equivalent indicators from the supply and demand perspectives permits an objective assessment of a destination's quality.

An increase in overnight stays or tourism revenues, reduced unemployment, and level of visitor satisfaction are indicators that are not in themselves sufficient to evaluate the quality of a destination.

The increase in overnight stays may result from lower prices, just as increased tourism revenues can be inferred from a greater number of visitors (even if average expenditure is less), a rise in prices (that may affect the destination's competitiveness over the medium-term), longer stays or higher average expenditure per capita in response to more attractive and sophisticated supply. The decline in unemployment may indicate precarious labour conditions or simply result from the destination's response to greater demand. Ultimately, satisfaction is a function of customer expectations, and without knowing what those are, cannot be objectively determined.

The indicators for destinations are relative and mutually complementary. Before analysing them it is advisable to ensure that the figures referred to have been estimated consistently, using market studies, an analysis of competitors, a benchmarking exercise or the establishment of realistic, historically based objectives.

It should also be recalled that not all destination actors carry the same weight in contributing to customer satisfaction. The influence of accommodation establishments is substantial and varies according to market segment (holiday or business). Other subsectors contribute relatively little to the level of quality perceived or to successful tourism experiences.

If starting from zero, a market study is the best way to obtain the information necessary to identify and measure a destination's attributes and the expectations of its customers. In cases where there are models or standards for reference, alternative tools can also be used, as will be discussed in chapter 9. The objective, in either case, is to obtain an *x-ray* of the destination's performance over time.

6.2   Evaluation of quality: audit and self-evaluation

Managing a destination quality system means regularly measuring its effectiveness. This is done by means of an audit, which may be internal or external. A reference model is needed in either case for standards or objectives defined by the destination itself.

Audit, in this context, refers to an external evaluation of the destination in relation to what is required by the reference standard, which is generally associated with certification or association with a brand name.

An internal audit is referred to as a "self-evaluation". Unlike an audit per se (an annual process at most), self-evaluations are mechanisms for systematically gathering and analysing information for use in continuous improvement processes. It is highly advisable to conduct these repeatedly to evaluate progress toward defined objectives. It may be enough to do so annually but, depending on the resources available, the ideal would be up to four times a year.

The process is undertaken in both cases with the help of a script or checklist, confirming, based on testimony and documentary evidence, the degree of effectiveness in implementing the quality system and analysing the management data and records generated by the system. It may require the taking of samples (water or sand from beaches, for example, to analyse quality), interviews with key actors or photographs.

To measure the quality of a destination, all of the data obtained on the supply side must always be complemented by and contrasted with demand side surveys. It is impossible to know the effectiveness of measures taken to improve the quality of the destination if we do not know how much it satisfies the expectations of demand; consequently, surveys need to assess both prior expectations and level of satisfaction.

Table 6.1   **Example of an evaluation list for snow destinations specialized in family recreation**

Skift for children (conveyor belt)	
Winter trails or paths (usable with child strollers or sleds)	
Instruction in winter sports, with classes for children	
Meeting place for instruction in winter sports in the main ski area	
Assistance for children at the resort, and the skiing area (outdoors/indoors/both)	
After-school space in the ski area, indoors in the winter season	
Ski area for children (Swiss snow kids village or similar)	
Skating area and skate rental	
At least 3 km of prepared sledding trails and rental of sleds	
At least 1 competition for children per week (open to all)	
At least 1 nocturnal gathering per week	
Recreational area with at least four elements (halfpipe, kicker, etc.)	
Rental of recreational equipment (snowtubing, snowbike, etc.)	
Indoor sports centre (as an alternative in case of bad weather)	
Curling/*Eistockschiesen* (form of curling) and rental of equipment	
Sleigh rides for children	
Free chairlifts/ski lifts for children up to 9 years of age	
Free chairlifts/ski lifts for young people up to 16 years of age	
Exclusive supply (for example, a restaurant for children in the complex, etc.)	

Source: Swiss Tourism Federation, Quality Programme, *Catalogue of criteria 2013–2015;* adaptation and translation of the original.

6.3   Definition of quality objectives

6.3.1   Quality policies and objectives

Working at the destination level involves negotiating a consensus among the actors involved in defining policies and objectives. To be effective, it is useful to focus each year on a limited number of priorities, according to real possibilities – in terms of the market and resources – without attempting to address all of the destination's complexity and scope from the very beginning.

The deployment of policies and dissemination of objectives requires communication with specific target audiences – the market, the host community, and different layers within the organizations – with coherent, motivating messages in the appropriate language.

Policies and objectives must be a function of the destination's tourism vocation, as defined by its *mission and vision*[1] and the tourism development model chosen. It should include:

–   An action area, such as improving satisfaction levels or increasing positive recommendations;
–   A concrete, quantifiable objective, such as a 3% improvement in a particular index;
–   The design of actions to be carried out; and
–   Conditions that need to be respected and that delineate scope of application (e.g. exclusively confined to convention tourism).

Policies and objectives are managed in four phases corresponding to the P-D-C-A cycle (Plan–Do–Check–Act, see chapter 7), extending to the destination's lower operating and organizational levels. Two approaches to this work, or a combination of both, are possible: a hierarchical approach (considering the weight of each subsector in constructing the satisfaction index); or a causal approach (directly attacking the grounds for, or services concerned by, the visitor's dissatisfaction).

6.3.2   Strategic options for the enhancement of a destination's quality

A tourism destination's strategic objectives in developing and enhancing quality need to balance economic, environmental and social concerns and should be developed in close coordination with local residents and actors. These objectives need to be clear, precise, limited in number, prioritized, viable and concerted.

Once the objectives have been decided, strategies need to be defined and necessary improvement measures need to be identified and prioritized. The resulting catalogue needs to outline fields of action according to the destination's products and needs, including:

–   The organization or development of tourism supply to adapt it to visitor needs;
–   Communication, promotion and marketing initiatives;
–   Awareness heightening activities;
–   Training plans to improve skills and knowledge;
–   Quality tourism activities with providers;
–   Definition of the most effective participatory, organizational and management formulas;
–   The management of tourism information to compile and process strategic data, evaluate market trends and self-evaluate the effectiveness of the measures taken; and
–   Management of information provided to potential visitors or signposting about the destination's tourism supply.

The destination should evaluate its own situation, define its own objectives and develop its own particular strategy.

---

1   *Mission* in the context of strategic marketing, is the sense and reason for being of an organization.
    Vision of the future pertains to desirable achievements, quantitative and qualitiative.

The areas for action should be outlined with a view to:
- Consistency with the destination's tourism development objectives and strategies for growth (qualitative development, seasonal growth, etc.);
- Consensus among destination actors; and
- Viability (as a function of quantitative and qualitative results and of the human, technical and financial resources available).

6.4   Quality attributes

6.4.1   The concept and types of quality attributes

We refer to quality *attributes* as the characteristics of a given product or service that define its quality as perceived by the customer and influence customer satisfaction. They may or may not be shared by different market segments and may refer to the tangible or physical aspects, organizational aspects, or attitudinal aspects of a service:

Quality attributes can be classified into six categories:
1. *Basic attributes* are those taken for granted: they increase dissatisfaction if not offered but do not increase satisfaction much if they are. Cleanliness is a good example;
2. *Neutral attributes* do not add value. At one time, hotels used to offer customers a daily newspaper, unsolicited. A study by Intercontinental Hotels and Resorts discovered that the initiative was well received when customers received their usual newspaper – but not when another paper was offered, especially a local one. Such amenities are referred to as "superfluous" quality. They do not provide value, they may require complex logistics and they entail an unnecessary cost;
3. *Questionable attributes* produce contradictory evaluations. According to a study by the technology consulting firm Forrester, people are returning to traditional travel agencies for the reservation of complex itineraries, since there are no portals in the Internet for managing them on an integrated basis. The Internet is synonymous with independence (in searching for information and opportunities or purchasing programmes) but many people still feel more confident and closer to the products if they have a brochure in their hands enabling them to work more comfortably than through automated purchase orders. Similarly, the tranquil surroundings of a destination may be interpreted as pleasing or boring;
4. *Contradictory attributes* produce positive values where they are not present and negative values when they are. There is a growing tendency to charge for customer services or amenities that used to be included, such as seat selection, catering or upgrades in the case of commercial aviation, which have led passengers increasingly to switch to low-cost airlines for short or medium distance flights. To offset the loss of value added, some companies have opted to introduce technological innovations;
5. *Manifest or complementary attributes* are those whose presence creates satisfaction in direct proportion to their functionality. For example, in the case of destinations, the use of modern information, interpretation and orientation devices, such as audio guides, automated information points or enhanced reality, while not strictly necessary, have a very positive effect; and
6. *Symbolic attributes* are those around which marketing promises revolve and which relate to latent aspects whose discovery and notoriety can become a competitive advantage if we are capable of adequately and consistently attending to them. Fashionable destinations depend

to a great extent on such attributes. They may be associated for example with design (Milan, Miami or Barcelona), lifestyle (slow cities), technology (the so-called "intelligent destinations") or creativity (UNESCO creative cities).

Identifying the quality attributes of processes, products and services is key to customer satisfaction and effective management.

Once a satisfactory quality level has been achieved and solidly maintained, attention to symbolic attributes can help to confront the challenges of the market by *surpassing* the clients' expectations, which requires a level of creativity and innovation not within the reach of every organization or destination.

The attributes that help to define the quality of a tourism destination have relative weights depending on the kind of destination and, to a lesser extent, on the market segment concerned. For example, noisy surroundings (the attribute would be quietness) are often unbearable for adults but part of a fun experience for young people.

6.4.2   What attributes are associated with a destination's quality?

Different studies concur in identifying key attributes that customers often associate with the idea of a quality destination. They are outlined below by order of importance.

Perception of security

The first quality attribute for any destination is personal security, whether real or perceived and whether associated with crime, with travel or transit or with the practice of tourism itself. An insecure or unsafe destination will not prosper. Fundamental security requisites include crime prevention, control of high-risk activities (and those who purvey them), road safety, as well as information and advisories about the risks of visiting certain attractions.

Security does not depend only on objective factors. It is also a subjective attribute. It is interesting, for instance, how inadequate lighting on deserted streets can create a sense of insecurity at urban destinations but not at rural ones.

The conditions at a destination are not the only cause of insecurity. It may also result from the reckless behaviour of visitors or imprudence on the part of tourism package organizers.

Working on security at a destination involves both prevention and the development of protocols to ensure effective action should security incidents nonetheless occur.

Other factors that affect perceptions of security are the hospitability of the host community and local providers, and information management. One feels more secure in a cordial environment. Cultural distance and language barriers have mistakenly led some countries to develop exclusive tourist resorts that hardly reflect the reality of the destination, instead of tackling the origins of their structural drawbacks as destinations.

The presence of police can create a sense of security – or anxiety if armed and wearing military-style uniforms. Some destinations have started programmes to raise awareness about tourism and security among law and order forces, together with training and image enhancements. Others have introduced special units to coordinate with local destination authorities and tourism value chain components.

Taking into account the concern it can generate, security management requires both discretion in making recommendations and clarity in the application of preventive measures. Some destinations and companies overdo it and create worries.

Case study 6.1   **Tourism Police (Colombia)**

Colombia is aware of the specific set of issues that surround security in tourism, the perceptions tourists have about security and how it affects their level of satisfaction.

Colombia has established a Tourism Police force *(Policía de Turismo)*, a specialized corps of its National Police that maintains a presence at tourism destinations and major attractions specifically for the protection of tourists. Its main functions include:

–   Providing orientation and information to tourists;

–   Raising awareness of, promoting and restoring values, traditions and a sense of ownership and respect for the country's cultural heritage;

–   Monitoring and controlling tourist attractions;

–   Overseeing compliance with legal requirements by local companies (such as registration with the National Tourism Registry); and

–   Eradicating drug trafficking and child prostitution associated with tourism.

The Tourism Police falls under the authority of the Vice Ministry of Commerce and Tourism and coordinates with other security forces, with national, regional and local authorities and with business organizations at major tourism destinations.

The Special Plan for Candelaria provides not only for the Tourism Police's monitoring and protection function but also its role as tourism information providers and guides for tourists visiting the old town centre in Bogota. This experience has been transferred to many other attractions and destinations. To carry out its functions the Tourism Police receives training on tourism legislation and regulations, as well as in providing information and tourist guide services and psychological training to know how to conduct themselves when tourists become victims.

The Tourism Police manages the following programmes:

–   *"Civiplayas"* ("civilized beaches"), to coordinate public and private sector efforts to improve beaches and enjoyment of the beach experience;

–   "Tourism Security Frontlines", in which individuals and public and private institutions promote better security for tourists and tourism service providers;

–   "Tourism Caravans – Secure Routes", to improve security for people traveling on Colombian roads;

–   "I Love My City", which coordinates the monitoring and control of tourist attractions in general with the local communities concerned;

–   "Information Stand" to provide information to tourists while monitoring and controlling national tourist attractions;

–   "National Tourism Registry", for use in awareness raising campaigns and the enforcement of the legal obligations of tourism service providers; and

–   "Tourism Security Councils", regional advisory bodies that work in coordination with the relevant authorities in a facilitating and advisory capacity on matters of tourism security.

Recently, as part of its Tourism Security Strategic Plan, Colombia has developed security protocols for application in responding to disasters, in respect of security personnel, environmental risks, risks related to tourist services, health and sanitation, events and crowds, road and transport security, management of information and the preservation of natural spaces.

Sanitation and health

A second attribute, which is obvious but nonetheless important – to the point of conditioning demand – is health and sanitation. A lack of qualified medical services, for example, was long a factor that deterred families from trying rural tourism, which has since become their main market segment.

This attribute encompasses the availability of quality medical services and the absence of epidemics and related risks to health, food, water and the environment.

Some destinations lack the basic medical services needed to attend to or evacuate people suffering trauma, accidents, illness or poisonous bites. Such deficiencies, not notorious until an incident occurs, can be catastrophic for a destination's reputation when published and spread in the public domain, inflicting particular damage on emerging destinations, still struggling to gain market recognition.

Respect for the environment and human heritage

Attributes can also be recognized in small details or annoyances for visitors.

To humanize cities, the measures taken include limiting traffic, adding pedestrian zones and bicycle routes. In natural environments – forests or beaches, for example – quality is associated not only with the survival of the original environment, but also with the existence of facilities permitting rational, controlled and responsible use of it (such as information points, toilets, access for the disabled, zoning, accommodation appropriate for the environment). Mature destinations, such as those that emerged during the developmentalism of the 1960s, have made a considerable effort to adapt, with plans to convert obsolete tourism infrastructure into recreational space for visitors.

While there is growing awareness in this regard, not all tourists particularly care about how rationally the environment, natural or urban, is being developed. So it is more a cultural problem than one of supervision, respect for the environment, adoption of good practices or measures to reduce urban, atmospheric, noise, light or acoustic pollution at destinations.

Tourism management is an exercise in balancing quality against quantity. It is important to achieve the critical mass necessary for destinations and activities to be sustainable. Protection to the ultimate extreme is not compatible with tourism. But neither are cases where the authorities are not able to control the flows and effects of tourism activity. The best strategy is to educate local actors and visitors and appeal to a sense of shared responsibility. Tourists with greater awareness understand and are willing to accept some degree of discomfort or some limitations (such as quotas, use restrictions, or pre-established itineraries).

The dissemination of information on the measures being taken, the use of information panels and the repeated communication of key concepts to tourists (even through local guides and providers of basic services) reinforce the idea of commitment amongst the local authorities and community.

Resource and space planning

The factors that clearly work against the choice of a destination and that cause dissatisfaction include:
– Crowding and lack of privacy as a consequence of overdevelopment;
– Unbridled urban growth and construction;
– Congested beaches and streets;
– Poorly organized public spaces and event venues; and
– Supply failures resulting from poor planning of services for a floating population.

These are problems endemic to destinations that have opted for intensive tourism development models or that are subject to strong seasonality.

An interesting pattern observed, with regard to energy and water supply, is that tourists tend to expect levels of quality equivalent to that in their countries of origin.

Cleanliness from the objective point of view

This is a universal concern and includes cleanliness in tourist establishments and in destinations as a whole.

The perception always relates to an entire destination, without distinctions between providers and the surrounding environment, and is an unshaded black or white: a destination is considered either clean or dirty.

Things that can convey an image of cleanliness include:
– Taxi drivers' clothing;
– Cleanliness of public transport and public services;
– Maintenance of bus stops, signs and entrances;
– Lack of overflowing waste bins, excrement, cigarette ends and other litter on the streets; and
– The quality of water and beaches.

Harmonious destination quality

It is important that the quality of all of a destination's services be harmonious and contribute to an enjoyable experience.

Harmonious quality refers not only to maintaining comparable levels for different components of the destination's value chain (accommodation, restaurants, reception services, etc.; see preceding chapter) but also to aspects frequently neglected by emerging destinations, still lacking mechanisms to police them, such as visual, environmental or noise pollution.

Visits to some destinations call for behaviour consistent with their intrinsic value. Loud music, for example, is incompatible with natural settings. Commercial billboards or furnishing schemes can clash with the architectural heritage of historic (e.g. colonial) town centres.

Integrated supply: beyond the quality of accommodation and restaurant services

Among the intangibles that increasingly add value to any tourism experience, attractive destinations offer *complete* services and products. It is not enough to meet visitors' basic needs (eating, sleeping, moving about, etc.) or to offer the right resources (landscapes, monuments, etc.) if the necessary value is not given to them.

This is not about *sophistication,* since experience or *adventure* are associated with the characteristics of the receiving environment and community. On the other hand, certain basic technical requisites do come into play. Whether a destination or product is specialized or generic, *integrated* and varied supply can inspire visitors to stay, prolong their stay and spend more money.

Connectivity

The connectivity of a destination – accessibility to the destination and within it – is another quality factor that directly affects demand.

All of the studies pointed to this aspect as a key factor of competitiveness. Connectivity is not measured in kilometres but in travel hours. Hence, the distance between points, close geographically, can be great if the roads are in bad condition, if the supply and frequency of transport is limited or if getting there requires unreasonable travel connections. Even if a tourist is prepared to undergo certain hardships to reach a destination, including lengthy travel times, such tolerance is proportional to the interest that destination inspires.

A destination offering many virtues but poor accessibility is better at keeping its virginity intact, which paradoxically makes it more attractive. The more inaccessible a destination the greater a visitor's expectations, and the more limited the demand and possibilities for growth.

Honest prices and reasonable costs

To counteract the inflation generated as a result of tourism demand, which also affects the local community, some destinations establish two price ranges: one for local residents and the other for visitors. This practice is clearly unethical and can in no case be justified by a lack of official supervision. It is a practice as pernicious for the reputation of a destination as artificially doctoring its service costs.

Professionalism

Among the skills indicative of professionalism in the delivery of tourism services are the following:
–   Technical competence;
–   Language skills;
–   Efficiency;
–   Organization; and
–   Problem-solving.

Warmth, hospitality and respect for the tourist

This attribute represents a differentiating variable for destinations, irrespective of their technical performance or intrinsic attractiveness.

It comes from two sources:
1. The *local population,* in the form of a hospitable and open attitude toward visitors; and
2. *Tourism professionals,* in the form of friendliness, productivity and a dedication to service.

Hostility or discrimination on the part of the population results from or is aggravated by prejudices in respect of culture, gender and ethnicity, language barriers or excessive socio-environmental pressure caused by inadequate destination planning.

Accessible, exhaustive and up-to-date tourism information

Information about the destination is not only indicative of transparency but is also input for a destination's marketing sales pitch. Even in the case of tourists actively seeking information it is always good to proactively provide and promote activities and events and places of interest in the best light possible.

Information is a double-edged sword. It can serve as positive reinforcement of visitor satisfaction and be a key factor in selecting a particular destination rather than one of its competitors; but if absent, deficient, or out of date, it can generate concern and be a dissuasive factor.

Appropriate interpretation and signposting for attractions

This attribute strengthens a destination's attractiveness and enjoyability. It marks the difference between a *primary* tourism economy and an *advanced* one. Pointing out, providing thematic context, interpreting and integrating attractions helps to make them recognizable and easily marketable products.

Enhanced accommodation and restaurant services

These are the primary attributes of a destination's quality and where the user tends to perceive most clearly the value-for-price ratio. Aware that there are different price ranges, tourists experience frustration when the experience falls short of expectations; the value/price ratio can provoke emotions that range from *feeling cheated* to a sense of being treated *honestly.* Tourists often do not understand that the price of a hotel room for a single night can equal a waiter's monthly wages.

Sufficiency of infrastructure and public services

Tourists assess public services in unequal if relevant ways depending on the destination and their own particular circumstances. A crowded airport is the first image travellers receive and to some extent alerts them that essential services will cost more, since tourists tend to have negative perceptions of dehumanized frontier formalities, deficient public transport or poor signposting.

Negative attributes

Apart from defects in the attributes mentioned above, tourists usually refer to a series of factors as contributing to bad experiences at the destinations they have visited, which again, while obvious, are nonetheless important:

– **Inadequate public transport:** in the case of more autonomous visitors, transport tends to be one of the most sought after yet least appreciated aspects of their visits, at least in emerging destinations. Complaints usually refer to the condition and cleanliness of the vehicles, security, availability, reliability and frequency of service, driver rudeness, theft and overcharging. These problems beset both inter-urban transport and intra-urban transit, the latter being that most used by tourists.

– **Significant differences depending on the time of year:** the attractiveness of destinations varies according to the season. Some destinations, like Venice, remain attractive even in winter, for a different clientele. Others seem to languish in low season, with minimal supply, closed establishments and limited commercial and social activity. While not necessarily seen as a sign of poor quality, these things are perceived negatively by the visitor, whether aware of it or not when booking reservations for the trip.

6.5   Quality indicators

A *quality indicator* is a parameter or datum representative of an attribute the quantified measurement of which reflects the quality of a process. It is used to monitor processes in time and evaluate their effectiveness and efforts to improve them.

Several different indicators can correspond to a single attribute. Sometimes, attributes that are generically abstract become specific when they can be associated with indicators.

To evaluate an organization's performance with respect to quality, in terms of progress, setbacks, effective processes or measures, it is necessary to identify, select and correctly analyse all of the indicators in a systematic way. Indicators are tools for describing, projecting and predicting.

6.5.1   Types of indicators

When an indicator is constructed, reference is made to the fulfilment of an objective, an expectation or a requirement using a numerical value, a scale, a fraction of time or a percentage.

There are many kinds of indicator: of compliance or impact, of yield or efficiency, effectiveness or oversight, of effect, of management and of context (which are the ones used to analyse the socioeconomic characteristics of a market or sector).

From the general to the particular they can refer to the destination as a whole and to subsectors, processes, activities or products. How they are chosen and measured depends on the objective:

–   *Direct* or primary *indicators* are generated by direct measurement; indirect or secondary indicators require additional steps;
–   *Simple indicators,* based on a single measurement of the characteristic to be evaluated, and expressed in units, are the most widely used given their ease of application; composite indicators combine several measurements;
–   *Weighted indicators* take into account other, not necessarily economic, variables according to the importance of the quality failure;
–   *Specific indicators* of a process or activity and general indicators, applicable to the destination as a whole, such as the number of arrivals or expenditure per visitor; and
–   *Objective* and *subjective indicators* are a function of method.

Indicators can be associated with subjective attributes, like cleanliness, that tourists perceive and assess according to their own experience and habits. Some place less importance on hygienic practices and assess disorder and uncleanliness on the basis of low expectations. In the case of destinations, it is useful to associate these attributes with more concrete indicators, such as the absence of litter on streets, disagreeable smells, overflowing bins, etc.

There are numerous examples of simple indicators, such as number of complaints, number of thefts, hotel occupancy, visitor flows to a particular attraction, etc. Composite indicators include water consumption or waste generated per person, data that vary according to the season and that are generally considered matters of management.

Direct indicators are critical in evaluating the results we expect to achieve; indirect indicators are those obtained, for example, from a satisfaction survey. Some quality indicators are of an economic nature (e.g. average spending) or a social nature (e.g. growth in tourism employment).

Any process can be measured using indicators, even those in which intangible components carry great weight. Courtesy, for example, cannot be measured objectively. But it can be measured indirectly or subjectively through tourist surveys.

For an indicator to accomplish its function it has to be:
–   Realistic and scaled according to the quality of the process, product or service;
–   Easy to manage, measure, interpret and analyse;
–   Positive and quantifiable;
–   Sensitive, i.e. varying appreciably over time;
–   Objective, without leaving room for ambiguity;
–   Reliable, uniform and not a function of the environment (in the case of energy, for example, the indicator is not the cost but the consumption);
–   Concrete, so as not to be interpreted differently depending on who is observing it;
–   Flexible and adaptive to needs, either temporarily or permanently; and
–   Representative, significant for the visitor and the destination according to the objectives established, and subject to expression in economic terms.

It may be difficult to interpret the quality attributes of a destination using objective indicators, since the tourist experience is essentially subjective: it can be evaluated in many different ways, under identical circumstances, by different customers.

Although more than 350 indicators have been identified for destination management it is enough to apply around thirty of them, combining some that allow comparisons with other destinations (for example, employment in tourism) with others that permit analysis of the individual destination.

6.5.2   How to construct a table of indicators?

A dashboard or control panel assembling the most relevant indicators can be a very helpful way to visualize them clearly, usefully, simply, synoptically and in summarized fashion, showing trends in fundamental business parameters.

To be analysed correctly, the indicators brought together in the dashboard need to be interrelated and balanced since, from an economic perspective, no single indicator tells the whole story. For example, a destination that has shown positive growth in tourism income but also a high degree of saturation in terms of land use is in all probability headed toward a slowdown or stagnancy.

In the case of a destination, the indicators listed below are interrelated and represent different facets of the same reality:
–   Economic results (creation of supply, investment, tourism expenditure, domestic product, tourism employment and inflation);
–   Pressures on the local environment (consumption, waste, density, saturation, second residences, etc.);
–   Current conditions (water quality, assessments by the local population and visitors, supply interruptions); and
–   Tourism management response capacity (capacity for water purification, companies with quality certifications, selective collection of containers, tourism expenditure, participation in collective action).

The introduction of a system of indicators requires the establishment of a regulated mechanism for the regular collection and processing of data. Given the complexity entailed it may be more practical to focus attention on a limited number of priorities in representative areas pending oversight. The focus can be broadened as the system is consolidated and additional resources become available.

Table 6.2.   **Examples of the linkages between possible attributes and indicators**

Example	Attributes	Indicators
Railway, ports and airports	Connectivity of the destination	– Transfer times; – Connections; – Frequency; and – Distance to centre, etc.
	Capacity of the facilities	– Schedule delays because of traffic saturation; – Occupancy rate; and – Intensity/congestion of facility use, etc.
Retail and financial facilities	Adequacy of supply	– Volume (number of shops and surface area) per 1,000 population; – Number of tax-free shops; – Number of local craft shops; – Average weekly hours of business; and – ATMs/bureaux de change per 1,000 population, etc.
Equipment for tourism (by segment)	Capacity	– Available places; and – Occupancy rate, etc.
	Adequacy of supply	– Distribution by category; – Languages available; – Number of incidents and complaints; – Income; – Accepted payment systems; and – Selected processing times, etc.

6.5.3   Indicators by type of destination

This section covers a series of basic quality indicators for a tourism destination by type, to guide the process of definition. All refer to the period of measurement established. They need to be measured regularly and compared for equivalent periods of time.

Generic destination indicators

Generic destination indicators include:
– Number of visitors, excursionists and tourists;
– Average stay (days);
– Tourism expenditure by visitors and tourist/day (total and by segment);
– Days/year in which receptive capacity is exceeded;
– Number of visits for a determined period, receptive capacity/equipment;
– Investments (by type; ratio per tourist);
– Number of jobs created;
– Number of unsafety episodes: accidents and reports;
– Average response time of emergency services (hours);
– Number of infractions;

–   Number or duration of supply interruptions;
–   Execution of the Tourism Plan (%);
–   Number of declared resources of interest to tourism;
–   Investments in maintenance and remodelling, per tourist/year;
–   Land occupancy (% of total);
–   Green zones (% of total); and
–   Density (inhabitants/km^2).

Commercial indicators include:
–   Total number of information queries;
–   Adequacy, visibility and effectiveness of the information and signposting (survey);
–   Volume of service provided by information desks (average number of people attended/hour);
–   Total number of visits to the destination's web page;
–   Returns within a determined period of time (%);
–   Visitors who would recommend the destination (%);
–   Certified companies (% of total);
–   Satisfaction index (survey);
–   Number of complaints received (absolute or relative amount to total visitors/year);
–   Assessment of quality/price (survey);
–   Promotional budget per visitor (amount);
–   Average cost of attracting new visitors; and
–   Value of free promotion.

Sustainability indicators include:
–   Investment in awareness activities;
–   Business climate indices (survey);
–   Satisfaction indices (residents; survey);
–   Number of tourism enterprises with majority local ownership;
–   Energy consumption (kWh/person [residents and visitors]/period);
–   Water consumption (m^3/person [residents and visitors]/period);
–   Waste (kg/person [residents and visitors]/day);
–   Contribution of tourism to the local economy (% of GDP; income per inhabitant);
–   Concentration of CO_2 gases/period;
–   Surroundings (survey); and
–   Tax receipts generated by tourism.

Cross-cutting indicators:
–   Professionalism: aggregated customer assessments for the different subsectors (survey);
–   Cleanliness and maintenance: as assessed by the customer (survey);
–   Accessibility: adequate facilities (% of qualifying establishments);
–   Hospitality and friendliness: as assessed by the customer (survey);
–   Health: healthcare centres, beds, ambulances and pharmacies (number/1,000 inhabitants); and
–   Security: police stations; police personnel and vehicles (number/1,000 inhabitants).

Specific indicators by type of destination

Natural/rural spaces:
- Marked trails/total km;
- Accessible trails/total km;
- Number of visitors to nature centres;
- Financial contribution of tourism to conservation (amount);
- Human resources for administration and maintenance (people/ha); and
- Sanctions (number/period).

Urban areas/heritage:
- Protected heritage: inventoried sites, buildings, etc. (% de infrastructure protected/total);
- Investment in restaurant services supply (absolute);
- Heritage resources adapted for visits by the public (% of total);
- Resources destroyed or declared at risk (% of total);
- Street furniture: units (absolute value) and assessment (survey);
- Overall harmony: value as assessed by the customer (survey); and
- Parking places (number/1,000 inhabitants).

Beaches:
- Facilities: availability of dressing rooms, showers and toilets (number/m^2 of beach);
- Certified beaches (% of total);
- Services: hammocks, umbrellas for hire (units/m^2 of beach);
- Biotic conditions: results of chemical-biological analysis of sand and water;
- Restaurant services: value as assessed by the customer (survey);
- Training: courses, students, hours offered; and
- Number of transits through recreational ports.

Ski:
- Wait time for lifts (minutes);
- Wait time at ticket windows (minutes);
- Wait time for rentals (minutes);
- Parking capacity (days/year in which capacity is exceeded);
- Number of points providing information about slope conditions;
- Number of restrooms and toilets within the skiable area;
- Training: courses, students, hours given (ski schools);
- Usable slopes (average km); and
- Assessment of *aprés-ski* supply (survey).

Specific indicators of a destination's supply

Accommodation:
- Occupancy (% of total/period);
- RevPAR (income/room);
- Standard deviation from average annual occupancy;
- YIELD (real occupancy/potential occupancy);

- Accommodations under partial or total remodelling (% of total);
- Modernization of facilities (annual amount of major investments in remodelling/rooms at the destination or time intervals between major remodelling);
- Training (by competency) per employee (hours/year);
- Stability: staff turnover (average % of total); and
- Languages (% of total personnel with additional language).

Restaurant services:
- Average price per client;
- Average cost per client;
- Training (by competency) per employee (hours/year);
- Stability: staff turnover (average % of total);
- Establishments food hygiene system (% of total);
- Languages, menu and personnel (% of total); and
- Supply of local gastronomy (% of total menu offerings).

Active tourism enterprises:
- Ratio of accidents or dissatisfaction/customer served/company;
- Training (by competency) per employee in hours/year;
- Stability: staff turnover (average % of total); and
- Languages (% of total).

Transport:
- Occupancy (seating: % of total supply), frequency (average wait time; minutes);
- Quality: assessment (survey);
- Punctuality: average delay (minutes);
- Average age of fleet (years);
- Training (by competency) per employee (hours/year);
- Stability: staff turnover (average % of total); and
- Languages (% of total).

Complementary supply:
- Adequacy (survey);
- Shopping (m^2/1,000 inhabitants);
- Variety of commercial supply per client (survey);
- Shopping: business hours (hours/year);
- Number of crafted products with denomination of origin;
- Shopping: establishments accepting credit cards (% of total);
- ATMs: number/1,000 inhabitants; and
- Recreational areas: number/1,000 inhabitants.

Supply conference/incentive tourism:
- Level of occupancy of conference rooms (% of seating and total supply);
- Attendants (number/year);
- Events (number/year and rate of materialization);
- Average expenditure; and
- Assessment of efficiency by convention bureau members (survey).

6.6 Quality standards

Quality standards refer to the level of quality that an organization desires to attain and has set as an objective. Reference is made to a standard already defined for the sector concerned or established by a third-party (an association, standardizing entity, brand or public administration).

The standards differentiate between organizations and destinations.

Despite the practical difficulties entailed in concerted action and compromise among actors, destinations actively pursue the establishment of standards for their supply of products and services, to the extent that they can become differentiating elements, as in the case of brands, "tourism product clubs" or thematic routes (such as the one dedicated to cheese in Bregenzerwald, Austria).

An example of a quality standard for a destination is a visitor quota and limited visiting hours for fragile tourism resources; or maximum wait times for customs and immigration formalities upon arrival.

6.7 Good practices

The introduction of good practices is a simpler way to define quality standards without having to refer to a standard. Their adoption can be useful in cases where:
– There is a need to implement quality at very large destinations;
– There is a need to generate results and a demonstrator effect in the market over the very short term, since simplification of the system and entry and recognition requirements favours participation;
– The destination's actors do not have the knowledge or awareness required, and a *re-education* process might be introduced;
– The organizational and economic resources are limited, either by the promoter (lack of public budget) or beneficiaries of the initiative (inadequate audit and certification processes often hampers microenterprises and small and medium-sized enterprises (SMEs); and
– A cost-benefit analysis needs to be performed when the destination develops a quality plan. For example, at rural destinations the geographical dispersion and size of companies increases the costs, making it hard to justify major investments with questionable returns to simplify organizational and productive processes.

6.8 Destination quality management

6.8.1 Processes and procedures

The distinction between products and services is not always clear-cut. All products have tangible and intangible components (brand, after-sales service, etc.). When the latter are the principle components, we call it a service, but both are the result of a series of concatenated activities performed by organizations and destinations that we call processes.

Standardizing a process of an organization or destination consists of setting and generally applying homogeneous levels of value delivered, applying precise, pre-defined execution criteria to guarantee a satisfactory result that conforms to pre-defined specifications and standards. Quality standards are established according to prevailing quality norms or those established in quality policies and/or objectives applicable to the destination.

The processes can be:
– *Business-related:* if several organizational units are involved (as in the case of a package or the development of statistics for the destination);
– *Functional:* when a single organizational unit is developed (such as the management of information kiosks); and
– *Unit-based:* in the case of basic tasks or activities (such as those entailed for a tourism office in attending to the public).

When a functional process is described in writing it is called a *procedure.*

Achieving satisfactory levels of quality means planning and carrying out processes correctly. Products or services are made to satisfy customers by constantly improving processes, so new organizational models (in both companies and destinations) must be aimed at process management. Such a process-centred approach breaks down barriers, reinforces the core business concept, improves work flow, optimizes resource use, promotes teamwork and improves internal communication.

Destinations are multifunctional virtual entities. Dealing with the quality of the destination from an exclusively vertical or sectoral perspective can leave gaps in responsibility and therefore cause problems.

Process management is a methodology that concentrates on the identification, control, management and improvement of key processes – basic and strategic – to transform them into *quality processes.*

Key processes are those associated with the positioning and competitiveness of the destination. We can distinguish between: basic processes, which affect customers though they might not perceive it (as in the case of security); and strategic processes, which affect business (such as marketing). Given the importance of creating a positive first impression of a destination, for example, reception might be considered a key process, dealing as it does with migration procedures, currency exchange, information at arrival and local transport. Some destinations, on the other hand, finding it difficult to control the abusive rates charged by taxi drivers, do no more than display the *official* rates, which are all but ignored.

Case study 6.2   **Quality in Tourism (United Kingdom)**

Quality in Tourism is the voluntary plan developed and managed by VisitBritain, the entity that resulted from merging the British Tourist Authority and English Tourism Council. Its mission is to promote the destination and create value through a system of brands or marks.

Adherence to the new scheme is an essential requisite in order to benefit from and participate in the promotions, tools, studies and publications of VisitBritain.

The plan entails classification by means of stars and a special gold or silver insignia for providers that exceed expectations applicable to their category. Prior verification before this distinction is awarded and subsequent supervision of compliance with standards are performed through a mechanism that includes prior evaluation on an annual basis and visits by a "mystery guest", performed by an independent and accredited advisor. The cost is covered by membership fees.

Tools have been developed to support the implementation and dissemination of this plan (consisting essentially of good practice guides, models and formats). Promotional activities and courses have also been developed.

The plan includes the definition of criteria for hotel and non-hotel accommodations (including campgrounds), centres of tourist interest that can be visited (castles, churches, museums, theme parks, interpretation centres, etc.) and boats, thus covering most of the tangible components that can be experienced by customers.

The evaluation is based on a number of minimum requisites that must be met according to each category, covering such essential aspects as security, hygiene, legal compliance, as well as standards of cleanliness or visitor information. Scores are determined according to intrinsic quality, maintenance, appearance, comfort and attention to detail or variety. The standards pay special attention to accessibility and adaptation for specific market segments, such as hikers or cyclists.

In parallel, VisitBritain has developed Quality Clubs targeting lucrative market segments, such as youth, gays and lesbians, or thematic initiatives based on luxury, culture or national heritage.

6.8.2   Documentary quality management

The enforcement of a *quality system* requires a minimum of documentary support. It need not be so exhaustive for destinations as for companies, but should at least cover the area of focus, objectives, key and common procedures, and records documenting implementation and results.

Documenting the quality system is important for the necessary purpose of organizing and standardizing work and avoiding random behaviour and mistakes.

The benefits of documenting processes include:
- An introspective analysis of the organization and its functioning;
- The structuring of processes;
- A documentary record of the data and information on hand; and
- Its availability for consultation as a source of guidance.

Generating *records* is part of quality control and measurement. In contrast to procedures, which do not normally change frequently, records are dynamic.

Procedures should be developed jointly by the people, the entities directly involved and the DMO, the supervisor of the process. In some cases, the use of images may facilitate understanding.

An example of a procedure for a destination would be the definition of security protocols establishing the sequence of actions that should be carried out and the responsibilities to be assumed. Another example is the definition of criteria to be followed by visits to specified vulnerable places to avoid negative impact or dissatisfaction for lack of organization or an excessive number of visitors.

Examples of records include surveys, inspections of business establishments, complaints, and recount procedures following access to tourist attractions.

Controlling the documentation of a quality system is a major organizational challenge and requires a systematic approach, including the use of numbered versions, creation dates and distribution lists.

Making access to this documentation easier is essential to the quality process. It is advisable for destinations to stage workshops to resolve any doubts, because not all entities or their staffs will have been able to participate in drafting the procedures and may not have the knowledge required to apply them.

6.8.3   Quality as assessed by customers

Image, trend and satisfaction studies help to more thoroughly understand customer expectations and to differentiate between the products and services offered.

Studies and surveys often prove defective because:
- The samples (those surveyed) are not selected methodically, such that the findings are not representative and the response rate is not high;
- Destinations use not qualified own personnel or students to conduct the surveys, rather than professionals, reducing the cost but compromising the results;
- The questionnaires are lengthy and dry, and the questions are confusing, such that aspects that are truly key for the customer cannot be prioritized; or
- The visitor's time is not appreciated or compensated, such that the survey is perceived as an annoyance; compensation need not be economic; perhaps the best thing to do is to show that the evaluation is appreciated and that the suggestions of those surveyed will be considered.

Complaint and suggestion systems allow for an immediate reaction. The fundamental keys are competence and quick responsiveness. The documentary support should be attractive and easy to fill out, given the high-pressure atmosphere such situations tend to create.

Case study 6.3   **The Tourist Advocate, Buenos Aires (Argentina)**

The Tourist Advocate is an autonomous institution under the Ombudsman's Office. Its activities are backed by the law and its supporting instrument is the Constitution of the Autonomous City of Buenos Aires, which establishes equal rights: tourist/travellers are equal to citizens, as in the slogan *"Un turista, un porteño" (A tourist, a "porteño" [inhabitant from Buenos Aires])*.

For the last ten years, the Tourist Advocate has been informing, accompanying and assisting tourists. It is a free service whose principal functions are to:

- Provide legal advice on the rights, guarantees and applications of tourists visiting the city or the Argentine Republic;

- Provide information enabling tourists to direct their questions and concerns via the fastest and most effective channels;

- Deal at the tourist's request with any complaint regarding the violation of a right or guarantee, using the fastest communication channels available for that purpose; this usually means processing lawsuits filed against hotels, travel agencies, passenger transport companies and businesses;

> – Refer matters to appropriate local or national agencies; company claims and tourist complaints that exceed the Tourist Advocate's authority or that are not resolved to the tourist's satisfaction. In the latter case the Tourist Advocate also assumes responsibility for monitoring subsequent action and keeping the tourist informed; and
>
> – Take the initiative to issue recommendations to official agencies, private companies or individuals, providing valid antecedents for subsequent judicial action.

6.9   Quality costs vs non-quality costs

Implementing a quality system entails a cost. This *quality cost* must be distinguished from the *cost of lacking quality,* which is less evident and is generally difficult to calculate.

Many organizations lack conviction in tackling quality and often mistakenly regard a certain percentage of mistakes and complaints as an acceptable routine. Nothing could be further from the philosophy of quality, one of whose greatest and clearest benefits is cost reduction.

80% of all quality failures take place in the initial phases of delivery, as a result of design flaws.[2] They then generally recur. As the process moves forward the costs accumulate and the failure is ultimately detected by customers. Herein lies the importance of quality systematization in the product design and planning phases. A good example would be a miscalculation in scheduling an excursion or tour, generating delays, losses and dissatisfaction, perhaps beyond economic compensation.

Table 6.3   **Examples of quality costs compared to non-quality costs**

Costs associated with quality	Costs resulting from non-quality
– Adequacy to the system's requirements;	– Failure to optimize resource use;
– Training;	– Duplication and repetition of tasks;
– Advisory assistance;	– Failure to resolve problems or complaints;
– Management;	– Poorly designed or executed promotions that require attention;
– Communication;	
– Changes in processes;	– Damage to competitiveness and image;
– Investment as necessary;	– Economic dependence for the destination;
– Client loyalty-creation;	– Loss of traditional activities;
– Innovation;	– Cultural deficits or environmental impact; and
– Prevention;	– Costs caused indirectly (owing to supply interruptions or equipment failure).
– Maintenance; and	
– Adaptation to meet regulatory requirements, including inspections and controls performed by the administrations.	

---

2   Rust, R. T.; Zahorik, A. J. and Keiningham, T. L. (1995), 'Return on quality: Making service quality financially accountable', *Journal of Marketing.*

The costs resulting from poor quality are estimated at about 40% of service company billing,[3] and in the specific case of tourism can account for up to 35% of income[4].

Quality failures that could generate costs include, among others:
−   Raw material shortages;
−   Losses;
−   Preparation of reports on compliance failures;
−   Guarantees executed;
−   Lower sales resulting from delays in the designs;
−   Defective maintenance;
−   Overrun caused by poor management of supplies;
−   Low productivity;
−   Reduced value of sales;
−   Improperly selected personnel;
−   Adaptation of software;
−   Repetition or duplication of tasks;
−   Attention to complaints;
−   Employee absenteeism;
−   Obsolete working methods and resources;
−   Losses in litigation;
−   Additional costs for insurance premiums and policies;
−   Fines;
−   Loss of customers;
−   Financing for amounts not paid;
−   Compensation;
−   Loss of reputation; and
−   Opportunity costs.

The costs associated with poor quality also affect customers, in two ways:
1.   Economic, in terms of the price paid and services received, such as loss of business resulting from flight delays; and
2.   Non-economic, such as time dedicated to presentation of a complaint, or stress, as in the case of time off work caused by intoxication.

The benefits of quality are therefore based on the relationship established between the costs of quality as compared with the costs of non-quality. The ratio between the two is 1:7. In other words the capital investment required to introduce a quality system generates a theoretical sevenfold return.

3   Peters, T. (2002), 'Reinventando el trabajo: las claves de la productividad', *Nowtilus,* ISBN 84-932527-2-7.

4   Gorga, V. (1999), 'Una aproximación a la calidad turística en el plano internacional', *Revista de Estudios Turísticos.*

6.10   Common challenges to destination quality

Inevitably, implementing a destination's quality system also means taking a series of measures that amount to the same old recipe:

- Diversification;
- Singularity and differentiation;
- Extended seasonality;
- Training policies;
- Effective human resource management; and
- Social integration.

The challenge is to actually make these things happen.

Studies have identified some more specific structural problems that are common to different types of destination, more specific and of diverse origin in addition to the quality attributes indicated above.

For instance, infrastructure breakdowns at conventional sun & beach destinations are generally associated with strong seasonality and high peak occupancy rates; tourism development and planning in rural areas lags behind because of geographical isolation, inexperience and the scarcity and dispersion of resources of all kinds. Different destinations will require different strategies.

The first common problem is related to the *management and maintenance of tourist attractions,* and often results from a lack of resources or poor coordination among the entities responsible for them. Neglect of their appearance as perceived by tourists could contribute to negative stereotypes and cultural colonialism. These attractions are often located in town centres and their management comes under not only tourism and culture departments but also urban planning and other departments, as they are an important part of life in the city. Other times, their geographical extent, as in the case of nature reserves (e.g. the great Amazonian reserves), the surrounding conditions, poor accessibility or lack of constant and adequate visitor flows make supervising and preserving them logistically complex, and require constant investments.

Another common problem is *breakdowns in infrastructure and public service during high season.* Seasonality in tourism activity damages the quality of services provided. But in addition, when essential services such as transport, security, cleanliness or healthcare are overwhelmed the destination's reputation is negatively impacted, regardless of whether visitors have used these services. Curiously, at many destinations, public services are planned on the basis of standard demand, to the point that it is frequent for employees to take their holidays just when tourists are arriving at peak levels. In other words, services are planned according to national uses and not the necessities of the market.

A third problem is a *lack of qualified personnel with foreign language skills.* While access to positions of responsibility is difficult in emerging destinations, mature destinations resort to immigration to cover basic jobs, with consequent problems in terms of integration and training.

The last, and perhaps most important, problem in some destinations is a *lack of hospitality.*

Case study 6.4   **Quality Tourism Plan, Andalusia (Spain)**

The quality tourism plan for Andalusia, 2010-2012, is the fruit of consensus among the public and private actors that intervene in that region's tourism sector. It proposes a new model for growth in tourism, promoting a business culture based on sustainability and responsibility, as well as a new stage in the management of tourism destinations, where innovation and excellence are combined to ensure the region's competitive capacity.

The plan includes 12 programmes and 49 activities, including training and participation mechanisms. With regard to destinations it proposes the introduction of integrated management strategies, initiatives to beautify the surroundings, actions to raise awareness about tourism and anonymous evaluation of the supply of services and products.

It provides for two communication and awareness campaigns: one for residents "Make Yourself at Home in Andalusia", and another for businesses "Efficiency in Business".

In order to recognize the commitment shown by companies, the plan:

–   Promotes certification;

–   Publishes a guide to certified entities and areas;

–   Creates a catalogue of good practices; and

–   Administers a prestige mark and a product club.

Chapter 7

The culture of quality and the human factor

Summary   This chapter examines the concept of quality as a management model associated with a culture whose development requires the concerted support of destination actors and tourism sector employees, since the human factor is the principal "hardware" of the tourism business.

Key words
- Continuous improvement; and
- P-D-C-A cycle (Plan–Do–Check–Act).

Key message   The culture of quality is based on six elements:

1. The customer-provider relationship, with the destination's customers understood as local actors, employees, other government departments and local society;
2. Causality, such that taking action to address a problem means understanding what has caused it, to prevent its repetition;
3. Continuous improvement as a systematic and planned process designed to improve the destination's services, products, processes and results;
4. Use of the P-D-C-A cycle as a constant to ensure the consistency of all implementation or improvement processes;
5. The work of transforming data into information, drawing on the knowledge generated to make substantial improvements; and
6. Recognition of effort, giving priority to processes and perseverance.

The human factor that enters into the quality of a host community's service and hospitality is the essence of the tourism business. The implementation of quality therefore requires refinement of the mechanisms for promoting the awareness and participation of relevant actors and development of the society's culture of hospitality.

All of this requires radical changes to current business models.

7.1   The culture of quality

A *culture of quality* is based on six indispensable elements that are associated with a specific kind of mentality:

1. Customer-provider relationship;
2. Causality;
3. Continuous improvement;
4. The P-D-C-A cycle (Plan–Do–Check–Act);
5. Attention to facts and figures; and
6. Recognition of effort.

7.1.1   Customer-provider relationship

Quality management means understanding that customer satisfaction must extend to all the organization's or destination's activities, and not just the ones involving contact with the final or external customer. The concept must also extend to internal customers, which consist for an enterprise of departments, providers and personnel, and for a destination, of agents, employees, other government departments and local society.

All of these actors influence the delivery of quality in tourism and can be the cause of dysfunction, since viewing the destination holistically, they have a part to play in providing and adding value to the services provided.

7.1.2   Causality

When a problem appears, the natural tendency is to correct it as soon as possible, but only on few occasions do we think about the cause. Acting on a problem means understanding its origin so as to avoid its repetition. All quality methodologies and tools are focused on a meticulous analysis of processes, tasks, results and problems that need solving.

A culture of quality establishes that, so long as the source of a problem has not been identified and its cause established, the problem will remain uncorrected and will reappear when most inopportune.

7.1.3   Continuous improvement

In quality management we find two distinct types of improvement: those that result from research, development and innovation, and those resulting from *continuous improvement*, reached by small steps. The former require investment, specialization and organizational and technological changes; the latter require continuous effort, dedication and recognition in working towards perfection. Combined use of both allows the progress gained through research and development efforts to be consolidated.

Situations in which quality is found lacking are the point of departure for continuous improvement. Improvement means the organized creation of beneficial change. An improvement plan consists of a series of structured and planned activities that must be performed according to a precise methodology and designed to identify, develop, implement and standardize improvement projects.

Correcting a problem has to mean eradicating what caused it. Chronic problems do not sound alarms, as we have learned to live with them. That is why improvement plans require the intelligent use of available data to find and delineate problems and analyse their causes in depth. That way we can ensure that improvements perceived in the initial stages are not merely cosmetic, but substantial, firm and standardized.

The tourism sector is not generally inclined toward radical innovation, which tends to be a possibility only in large organizations, not destinations. The latter require a single approach and high levels of cohesion, commitment and organization among local actors. Continuous improvement, on the other hand, is easy and cheap to implement.

Continuous improvement is not a methodology: it is a permanent attitude of analysis and of seizing opportunities as they arise that is applicable to everyday activities, as well as problem solving.

7.1.4   The P-D-C-A cycle

The processes needed to deliver a tourism product or service consume most of an organization's or destination's human and economic resources. But processes in the tourism sector depend largely on people, and it must be remembered that people are not machines (and even machines make mistakes). What people do must therefore be continuously analysed and improved.

Also known as the "Deming wheel", the P-D-C-A cycle (Plan–Do–Check–Act) is applicable to routine work.

A culture of quality can be supported by the P-D-C-A cycle as a constant in all methodologies, tools and implementation processes, to ensure consistency. It is used not only in the initial stages: the cycle can be *rerun* according to the results obtained or for the purpose of standardizing or modifying activities, following the continuous improvement philosophy until excellence is achieved.

Application of the P-D-C-A cycle to everyday tasks entails three different sub-cycles depending on the conclusions reached:
1.   Maintenance;
2.   Correction; and
3.   Improvement.

Going through the complete cycle generates continuous improvement, an indispensable element of any culture of quality. Such improvement is driven by systematic application of the cycle to all of the processes and activities of the destination and the organizations residing there.

The development and implementation of a destination's quality system is at all times a P-D-C-A cycle.

Figure 7.1.   **Intersection between the P-D-C-A cycle (Plan–Do–Check–Act) and the itinerary for implementing a quality system**

Control, updating and continuous improvement

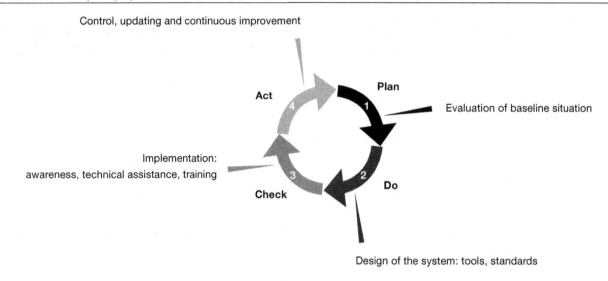

Evaluation of baseline situation

Implementation:
awareness, technical assistance, training

Design of the system: tools, standards

7.1.5   Working with facts and figures

Another component of the culture of quality is that decisions should be based on confirmable reality (facts and figures), not on intuitions or reflexes as often happens in the tourism sector. All information, both qualitative and above all quantitative, should be expressed in units of measurement according to the frequency of occurrence and used systematically. This means reviewing a destination's information and communications systems using indicators to evaluate performance. Experience shows that most of the necessary data exist but are often not evident or easily accessible. Gathering, processing and analysing data involves the use of specific tools. The challenge is to transform data into information and then draw on the knowledge generated to introduce real improvements.

7.1.6   Recognizing effort

In some cultures, quality and productivity are antagonistic concepts. The classic corporate model of recognition rewards quantitative results and rarely establishes quality objectives.

A culture of quality requires that recognition models give priority to processes and reward effort, which means training the people who will be conducting the processes and changing the relationship between management and employees, in terms of developing their capacity and motivating and empowering them, thus reducing the need for continuous control.

The recognition of effort is based on a compact among the various tourism actors with a view to achieving defined objectives and monitoring progress in doing so. In implementing its quality plan the destination will have introduced mechanisms for recognizing the commitment and effort of people, as well as companies (mainly certification in the latter case). Certification, awards and product mark/guarantees are often bestowed for a limited time and can only be renewed by demonstrating positive performance and continuing compliance with the standards or objectives concerned and a positive tendency.

7.2   People: essential hardware of the tourism business

The "hardware" of the tourism business, when it comes to delivering quality service, as well as hospitality on the part of host communities, consists of human beings.

Instilling quality means perfecting the mechanisms for raising awareness among and encouraging the participation of employees and other actors according to their capacity and knowledge. For a tourism destination quality means developing a culture of hospitality in the society and adopting a *common language* to that end. It may also mean a change in the models being applied.

7.2.1   Human capital

Tourism service is essentially of a personal nature. The quality of a service, however, cannot be understood as something random, arising only from the initiative or mood of individual professionals involved in the process.

Quality is a management model and a specific form of work that requires a concerted effort on the part of management, employees and destination actors. This model may seem subversive to those who still believe in organization models based on controlling salary costs (which have not proven competitive over the long term) as opposed to the development of opportunities and capacities.

Quality also means recognition and positive leadership, as opposed to the authority that derives from a *position,* as well as the commitment and contributions of the employee as a key figure in achieving the objectives and returns pursued. It is what is known as the Good Service Cycle[1]. Irrespective of his or her level of responsibility, motivation and dedication, the employee's contribution is fundamental to the management and improvement of quality.

That is why any change must start with people and turn afterwards to methods.

Service quality is not necessarily bad if staff wages are low, nor good if they are high. It seems paradoxical, however, that the people most important in maintaining an organization's or a destination's good reputation – those on the front lines – are often the most poorly qualified, the worst paid and the least committed. A number of analyses have concurred in identifying the quality of tour guides, for instance, as a critical factor (40%) in the satisfaction of tourists opting for packages and guided tours.

In the traditional, pyramid-shaped model, for managers (and politicians), the higher one reaches in the pyramid, the further one is removed from the customer, to the point, often, of being oblivious to the realities of daily management, whereas staff – on the *front line* in particular – accumulate a

---

1   Shlesinger, L. A. and Heskett, J. L. (1997), *Service Profit Chain,* Simon and Schuster (ISBN 9781439108307).

valuable body of first-hand information. The situation is no different at the level of the destination: "awareness" programmes are promoted for the staff, but local authorities, entrepreneurs and managers rarely participate in them.

Given the importance of staff to service processes – and the fact that staff is the easiest and least expensive factor of production to modulate, and the most effective in terms of short-term results – it is surprising how little importance is given to training in the tourism sector, where it tends to be regarded as a recognition tool or to be focused on technical knowledge rather than skills. In a changing and uncertain competitive environment, training means capacity to adapt.

It should also be considered that having to supervise all delegated tasks represents an avoidable expense. Making all decisions at high levels of management leads to detachment. Empowerment, based on the principle of responsibility and eliciting the best from each individual, generates motivation and commitment. It means delegating to, trusting and giving people a sense of ownership of their work. This kind of empowerment can help to offset the difficulty of controlling service processes that are of an immediate, real-time nature.

A destination cannot achieve high quality if the companies operating there do not apply these simple precepts.

7.2.2   Hospitality

"The quality of the visitors' experience is related to their complete satisfaction, derived from a unique experience consisting of personalized and efficient services and real interaction with the receptive community's culture". So says the *Breviary of Tourist Culture,* published by Mexico's Ministry of Tourism (SECTUR – Secretaría de Turismo). Experience is the interpretation of what happens to the visitor, and when feelings and emotions enter into play, leads to reflection that goes beyond what is observed.

Societies, like organizations, rely on explicit codes, which are nothing other than a manifestation of their ideological, behavioural and material systems. Sometimes these systems clash culturally with the values shared by tourists, particularly those pertaining to religion, social behaviour and language.

A tourism destination can never truly thrive if the local community lacks a sense of hospitality. The host community needs first of all to be aware of the characteristics of tourism activity and the stakes involved, which means:
–   Being sufficiently sensitive to their visitors' particularities, needs and motivations; and
–   Recognizing the economic benefits derived from the cultural interaction generated by tourism.

This can be achieved through a communication campaign reaching all strata of the local population (including schools in some cases) to help instil honesty, respect, responsibility, a vocation for service, friendliness, a willingness to help and professionalism.

But it is also important to establish indicators of sustainability to protect native values, not only for ethical reasons but as a simple matter of business continuity.

Case study 7.1   **Cooperation Model (Malta)**

In developing the strategic plan for tourism, the Tourism Authority of Malta found it necessary to update existing legislation to keep pace with the market requisites of the times and also to foster the implementation of quality in the interest of long-term business sustainability, strengthening the image and competitive positioning of its products and infrastructure for inbound tourism. The aim was to develop a comprehensive framework for the entire sector, to serve as the basis for a long-term improvement plan. It is a mixed approach that combines obligatory and voluntary tools.

As part of this process, obligatory and voluntary classification systems were introduced for the sector, the latter for businesses wishing to differentiate themselves in three ways:

1.   An insignia based on the special nature of their facilities (a historic building for example) or products (businesses, families, diving, etc.);

2.   Ecological labels for businesses adopting good environmental practices; and

3.   A quality label ("Hospitality Guaranteed") as recognition for a business's efforts to establish a quality management plan.

Such recognition requires an audit process whose implementation was facilitated with quality tools adapted to island realities.

The Directorate of Development Planning of the Tourism Authority of Malta is directly responsible for the design and installation of some product components, such as the organization of events and the beautification of surroundings (seaside promenades, for instance).

In addition, in cooperation with the local university there are plans to develop a programme for the creation of tourism spaces, in which development is combined with protection of the environment and interpretation centres inform visitors about a site's natural resources, history and architectural and archaeological heritage.

Chapter 8

Marketing quality

Summary   This chapter focuses on the mechanisms for quality recognition, promotion and communication.

Key words   – Brand;
        – Image;
        – Identity; and
        – Conformity mark.

Key message   Quality serves as an argument for the promotion and positioning of tourism destinations, since it permits strengths to be developed as competitive advantages.

The essential marketing tool for destination quality is the brand. Prestige marks and quality certifications coexist alongside commercial brands conveying a sense of excellence and reliability.

The cost involved in developing, positioning and promoting a brand is high, and thus not affordable for all destinations. Alternatives include adhering to an existing product certification system, network or club.

Quality can be recognized in two ways: prestige marks and conformity marks. The purpose of prestige marks is to separate the cream of supply. Conformity marks, which are generally voluntary, certify compliance with some existing standard. There are also marks based on values specific to a destination that can be used as recognition of quality, so as to make the destination itself the guarantee.

Communication activities strengthen a destination's identity. In parallel, the behaviour of institutions, businesses, and the local community, as well as a destination's economic and social conditions and the opinions of visitors and intermediaries, construct an image and reputation in a way that is totally uncontrollable.

The promotion of quality improves the destination's image externally while, internally, it represents an effort when sensitizing and mobilizing all destination actors.

8.1   The link between marketing and quality

It seems fair to argue that quality efforts made by destinations and companies deserve recognition. And yet, while not all variables in the communication process are under their control, the fact is that destinations usually neglect the promotion of quality as part of their communication efforts.

The main tool for marketing the quality of a destination is the creation of a brand. Prestige brands and quality certifications co-exist with commercial brands identifying companies. Not all are intelligible and fewer still are interesting to the public. The proliferation of brands in the tourism sector – sometimes to little effect – also generates confusion in markets and unnecessary and unproductive costs.

Quality control and marketing share the same objective, the same tools and a similar philosophy: the profitable satisfaction of customer needs.

Marketing complements quality in the identification and anticipation of customer requirements, the generation of demand, pricing and the creation of value-added, by making quality attributes a substantial part of the sales pitch and loyalty promotion effort. In attempting to take care of visitors – advise them, give them something more than a mere product, persuade them – marketing entails active management of quality as perceived by those customers.

The type and concentration of micro-organisms present in the water or sand of a beach or in a marina is a technical indicator not generally known to or understood by visitors. Visitors will tend to be guided by direct observation of such things as the presence of seaweed, traces of faecal matter or kerosene, overcrowding of bathers, presence of pets, the degree of supervision or vigilance or *Blue Flag*[1] designation.

A quality approach – adjusting programmed quality according to perceived quality – can turn strengths into competitive advantages.

8.2   The brand

The *brand* provides a visual identification of destinations, companies or products, and as such represents a strategic variable.

Brands can communicate a variety of differentiating values – lifestyles, attributes, etc. – vis-à-vis the competition. They are also defined as a function of different segments (price, service, specialty or location). A brand is considered successful when its image can capture attention and convey a clear, recognizable promise that consumers can associate with the product or service. Their effectiveness correlates in particular with this associative capacity.

When the consumer purchases a brand product there is an opportunity for differentiation and loyalty creation toward the brand. Branding also generates economies of scale.

The prominence of branding varies from one destination or sector to the next but is continually growing. For example, location (proximity to places of interest in the case of recreational travel, or to the office in the case of business travel) is the most important factor in selecting a hotel. However, in emerging destinations, unfamiliarity or apprehensions can make a well-known brand an important factor in selecting providers.

A successful brand has five key ingredients:
–   It must convey how good the product is;
–   It must be easy to pronounce, recognize and remember;
–   It must stand out;
–   It must not carry negative connotations in other cultures or languages; and
–   It must be registered.

---

1   *Blue Flag* is an insignia bestowed annually by the *Fundación Europea de Educación Ambiental* to beaches and ports meeting a series of environmental and facility-related conditions.

8.2.1 The development of quality marks

Quality is communicated to the consumer in the form of a graphic brand image, using a kind of *code* easily understood by the consumer. Brands do not belong to their promoters but rather acquire value when they enter into contact with the consumer. A brand's effectiveness is not simply a matter of being attractive but of the identification of that attractiveness with the real image, or that perceived by the tourist.

When recognized by a potential customer, the brand is an influence in the buying process.

Some countries have opted to develop a differentiated quality system of branding for destinations, businesses and products. The cost of developing, positioning and promoting a brand is high and not affordable for all destinations.

Prestige and conformity marks can be useful for the recognition of a product, business or destination.

8.2.2 Prestige marks vs conformity marks

Prestige marks and *conformity marks* can be promoted by private entities or public entities. Neither is exclusive of the other. Their use is subject to compliance with determined, theoretically relevant standards. They are regulated by means of contractual mechanisms that establish ownership, rights, uses and eligibility criteria.

When a prestige mark used to designate the quality of a product or business (AAA, Starlight, UNESCO Heritage, Biosphere, etc.) is well-positioned, it strives to become an emblem of excellence, specialization and commercial promotion. Consistent with that definition, prestige marks usually resort to intuitive comprehension (through the use of evocative symbols), as well as a careful, differentiated aesthetic. They are also used to identify product clubs.

While there are clearly defined filters for eligibility, prestige marks have more of a commercial aspect than conformity marks: their aim is to separate the cream of supply based on the distinctive characteristics that define them. It is therefore necessary to analyse what the brand offers to businesses or destinations and to consumers, what is required in exchange and what are the advantages relative to other possibilities.

If not profit-based, a prestige mark need not necessarily entail voluntary adherence; it can be awarded unilaterally by the promoting entity.

When the prestige mark is the result of a public initiative it is more exposed to scrutiny and the risk of failure – with possible political and economic consequences – for lack of tourism sector support gained through prior consultation and agreement. In addition, when sponsored for the purpose of strengthening promotion and generating a stimulative effect for supply, there is an ethical dilemma, since the prestige of a brand lies precisely in this exclusivity: not everyone can use it, and often, in order to avoid internal criticism about impartiality, the requisites for eligibility end up being lowered.

Only occasionally are they associated with mechanisms to improve quality or develop products or destinations strategically.

Examples of prestige marks:

Case study 8.1   **Travellers' Choice™ Awards**

The ranking done by TripAdvisor, the largest online traveller's community, is a marketing and recommendation tool. Members of its Internet forum can freely express their opinions about a destination or establishment, which are used to establish a ranking. Travellers' Choice™ awards are given to the best destinations, beaches, hotels and restaurants, although the assessments are a reflection of popularity, and not necessarily quality.

Conformity marks indicate compliance with a well-known and public standard or a quality standard. They are awarded by an accredited certifying authority or a public agency. Unlike prestige marks they are voluntary, accessible to all businesses without additional prerequisites and can sometimes arise from a business self-regulation process.

They establish minimum, never maximum or ideal, levels to be achieved. This lack of definition is their strength, enabling them to easily coexist alongside commercial brands.

Another of the characteristics that differentiate conformity marks from prestige marks lies in the use of diametrically opposed design criteria, since they are often aseptic, unsophisticated logos.

Examples of conformity seals:

Certification is often furthest advanced on the environmental front (pollution, energy efficiency, resource management, conservation of ecosystems, regional planning, environmental good practices) or social responsibility (management of tourism social and cultural affairs, fair trade, community development, the fight against sexual or child exploitation), as in the cases of Biosphere, Rainforest Alliance or Green Globe, among many others.

Examples of brands with environmental components:

8.2.3   Destination brand as guarantee

Some products or destination brands (Swiss Quality Seal, Madrid Excelente, Quality Tourism in Hong Kong, Gîtes de France, Brand Perú, etc.), generally regional or national ones, explicitly and graphically express values associated with the destination, which can be used as symbols of quality. The destination itself becomes the guarantee.

Destination brands applicable to businesses:

Ljubljanska
kakovost
2015

*Ljubljana
Quality
2015*

QUALITY
Our Passion

Case study 8.2   **Quality Seal of Approval (Switzerland)**

The challenge of competitiveness stimulated the creation of the Swiss Quality Programme based on certification of quality and the organization of quality clubs. Outstanding companies are awarded the Golden Flower, symbol of Swiss tourism.

In 2003, the Swiss government took a new approach with the Innotour Programme with the strategic aims of developing and improving its products, innovating in its processes and managing its costs efficiently.

The Innotour Programme includes a Seal of Approval, an example of certification associated with a destination developed by the University of Bern and the Frey Akademie with funding from the Secretary of State of Economy. Its aim is to foster awareness of quality in organizations and destinations. The Swiss Tourism Federation – one of the 12 organizations backing the scheme – has been entrusted with managing it, serving as chair of its Quality Council and providing a stable structure for the entity responsible for coordinating and controlling the Programme.

The organization of the scheme is complex because individual Cantons[a] are represented within it and also because it features working groups and regional quality assurance committees.

It is a multilevel system currently composed of 18 subsectors of activity, which can be expanded to achieve Total Quality for the most important stages. The levels are as follows:

Level 1, Quality of services, awareness and adoption of good practices. To obtain the Seal of Approval at this level the four instruments designed to support the programme must have been systematically implemented: service chains, quality profile, complaints and action plans.

Corresponding to the concept of "value chain", *service chains* are designed to heighten awareness about quality and communicate the need for destination-wide teamwork. Assistance is provided with practical implementation of quality, using indicators and the systematic review of processes and services to detect areas for improvement.

Under the heading of *quality profile,* the Programme reviews essential operational areas to determine the quality of services through a crosscutting and voluntary review of six of the eleven following sections:

– Awareness of customer expectations;

– Advanced staff training;

– Maintenance of materials and facilities;

– Awareness of customer experiences;

– Areas of special attention;

– Measurement of customer satisfaction;

– Measurement of staff satisfaction;

– Attention to customers;

– Correction of poor quality situations;

– Teamwork; and

– Cooperation with other associated hotels.

The programme requires the use of a questionnaire for complaints to evaluate how they are dealt with.

The areas identified as priorities for improvement by applying the three tools mentioned above are set out in a 12-month *action plan.*

For the implementation of quality management systems, businesses use qualified quality coaches and tools designed by the programme to simplify, extend and guarantee proper implementation, with the help of handbooks, presentations, audio-visual aids and remote external support.

The completed documentation is submitted for analysis to the Verification Unit. That unit's preliminary decision will be presented to the Regional Quality Commission, which is responsible for awarding the seal. After one year, businesses are required to review the results and update the action plan.

Level 2, Quality management refers to the implementation of a quality assurance system.

Level 3, Implementation of total quality management: the objective is development planned on the basis of tourism operations.

Achieving levels 2 and 3 requires additional training for company quality officers and the fulfilment of requisites of the corresponding level and is supported on the EFQM model to include the following requisites and instruments. The businesses assess their quality performance in the different organizational areas with the help of a guide. They systematically analyse the parameters of customer and employee satisfaction and receive the visit and evaluation of a "mystery customer" based on pre-established criteria. The results refer to the different types of logos for different specialities.

The programme has a special component dedicated to destinations, distinguishing between those specialized in families and those specialized in health tourism. The destinations conduct a self-evaluation which is then validated by an external audit.

There are some criteria that are common to both and that need to be addressed by the destination's tourism organization (such as information) and which generally require specific infrastructure, services and products according to the speciality.

Those specialized in families are assessed based on the presence of infrastructure such as children's playgrounds, recreational areas, lakes or swimming pools; stroller-friendly pathways, with themes and services, as well as custom-made products (horseback riding, family sports, cultural activities, facilitated programmes). Consideration is also given to the requisites concerning public transport (such as discounts or family vouchers), accommodation (safety features for children, appropriate housewares, space for strollers, menus for children, connecting rooms, etc.) and assistance at the destination (availability of caretakers, medical services, etc.).

Those specialized in health are assessed in terms of the services offered and the strategic orientation of the destination, the extensiveness of supply and qualified personnel.

The programme has distinguished 21 family destinations and 7 health tourism destinations.

---

a) Local governments; Switzerland is a federal State.

Destination brands applicable to businesses:

QUALITY
Our Passion

WELLNESS
Destination

GUEST ROOM
Holiday Comfort

FAMILY
Destination

The development of a quality destination logo tends to involve one or more of the following options:
–   The backing of a relevant international organization (such as the ISO, WTTC, UNWTO, UNESCO or EU) in developing certification schemes for destinations, equivalent to the ISO-9000 standards for companies – or linkage to existing certification schemes such as Green Globe or World Heritage Cities, which can provide structured content for a brand;
–   Use of the corporate identity of a destination as a quality mark, a strategy followed by the Tourism Authority of Malta to classify and certify conformity to a series of standards designed to distinguish between different levels of quality among the island's establishments, or based on existing, disseminated standards or reference points; and/or
–   Creation and promotion of one's own brand, generic or specialized, such as Q, created by the ICTE in Spain, or the Swiss Quality Seal of Approval.

All of these options generate positive synergies for the destination and any would be beneficial.

Depending on how the destination is defined as a product and the needs that it satisfies, it is important for the brand to be attractive and to evolve toward a kind of emotional discourse, in a credible and relevant way. It should focus on the destination's benefits for the customer, in terms of the quality, as well as the characteristics of supply. This not only enhances the brand's prestige but also provides a framework for relating to customers.

8.3   Promoting and communicating quality

Not all variables in the communication process are under the control of organizations or destinations and are sometimes even used by competitors or big operators to determine tourist flows. At the same time as the promotional and communication activities that the destination undertakes strengthen its identity, the behaviour of institutions, businesses and the local community; economic and social conditions at the destination, and the opinions of visitors and intermediaries all shape the image and reputation of a destination in a way that is totally uncontrollable.

The conditions of the destination and many of the conditions of its surroundings have a particular influence given the crosscutting nature and wide public exposure of tourism.

Quality is promoted and communicated both externally and internally:
1. Externally, through information and marketing processes and by improving the image of a product or destination, so as to increase the profitability of commercial transactions; and
2. Internally, as part of a sales effort, as well as a quality awareness, mobilization and training effort for all of a destination's local actors.

8.3.1   Quality promotional messaging

A market united by technology favours the marketing efforts of small- and medium-sized companies, facilitating their direct contact with potential customers, and allows destinations and providers to obtain feedback and consumers to transact with the operators of their choice. But it also means competing in a globalized market, where there are multiple options, where consumers are better informed, where commercial transactions are immediate, where communication tools are limited and where tourism providers and destinations lack control over the flow of information about them.

Far too often quality systems have been focused exclusively on technical improvements, with little regard for their effects on a destination's image. Associating the promotion of quality with promotion of the destination in general makes for a more tangible product. It also gives credibility and perspective to the values that differentiate the product or destination.

In this context, quality represents another link in the interaction and an argument for the purposes of communication. Applied to the processes of information and marketing quality requires guarantees of access to transparent, exhaustive, up-to-date, personalized and multilingual information.

Promotional communication with respect to quality consists of providing information about the quality system directly to consumers, tourism intermediaries, opinion leaders, through the adoption and dissemination of a series of arguments that explain and sell the benefits provided. It means using a solid line of work, avoiding gaps in communication and confused messages and adapting content to the interests of different target audiences.

A product, organization or destination perceived as one of *quality* will always be better positioned when purchases are made. When convention bureaus and film commissions compete to host conferences, incentive travel, sporting events or film shoots they highlight the facilities they could provide and call special attention to the attributes that reflect the quality of the destination.

If a customer is satisfied and confirms that the promise of a destination engaged in a quality process corresponds to the actual experience, loyalty is assured and the impact of promotional communication is multiplied.

Quality makes it possible to transform uncomfortable situations into advantages: any work to remodel and improve the destination is bothersome but if properly managed (to minimize its impact on the customer) and properly communicated, it conveys an impression of improvement and dynamism and commitment to the tourist.

To communicate quality it is essential, first of all, that both the generating and receiving markets understand the scope and significance of applying a quality system to tourism, which is not always the case. In communicating about quality, it is preferable to clearly enumerate the characteristics the customer can expect rather than generalize.

Given the scope entailed, the promotion of any quality plan or system is complex. In communicating about initiatives underway and progress made it is better to break the information down into several points:
–   Data on economic returns for the destination or data extracted from surveys (such as visitor preferences and satisfaction);
–   Position in the rankings, awards and distinctions;
–   Innovative products;
–   The successes of local entrepreneurs; and
–   Positive social impact, etc.

Prestige mark certification or adherence is only one milestone in a destination quality plan. This strategy allows for a continuous supply of information that is measured out over time.

To create its own certification and associated brand, a destination would have to plan the conceptualization, management and communication entailed. The costs of development, market positioning and promotion are significant, so this option is not affordable for all destinations. Alternatively, there is the possibility of resorting to pre-existing certification systems, at the national or international levels, or of joining a product network or club.

In choosing certification as a marketing tool, it should be considered that not all certification systems have the same impact on the public. With respect to businesses, it is not easy for customers to perceive what lies behind such widely used quality certifications as ISO-9000, and how they are benefited by them directly. They are accepted and have proven useful, however, in business-to-business relations.

8.3.2   Selling quality internally

This is about raising awareness among providers, authorities and local populations, encouraging their voluntary adherence to quality standards and creating the right conditions for the implementation and dissemination of quality.

The internal sale of quality requires a convincing sales pitch on the benefits of implementing quality, favouring participation and involvement in the design phase. In the initial phase the heads of organizations need to be persuaded that this need exists and to act accordingly.

To ensure that organizations and people get involved, their contributions must be taken into account and they must be informed continually about the plan's progress in proportion to their contributions, responsibility and positions. Where resources are limited the communication instruments of the plan can be supplemented by creating a special subheading for the instruments the destination and organizations usually use.

It is important to bear in mind, in the case of destinations, that the adhesion process is not always even. Many organizations emulate the participation of others, so it is useful to raise awareness and recruit in successive waves. Once the organizations initially incorporated are working on implantation and obtain significant results, a cascade effect will take place, building up the necessary critical mass to transform results into representative improvements throughout the destination. Particularly in the case of a voluntary plan or system, the extent of participation must be sufficient to ensure representativity and sustainability. In no case, however, should the process be forced, because the abandonment of any improvement could have much more negative effects.

Although the importance of implementing quality may be recognized by all actors, few organizations approach the process voluntarily with their own resources, or even have the necessary resources. Administrations therefore need to adopt tools for providing financial and technical support, which means essentially subsidies, advisory assistance and promotion.

Certification can also be linked to certain benefits so that organizations will be motivated to join: additional points for gaining access to public assistance, inclusion as a requisite for contracting with the administration, preferential promotion activities, etc.

Case study 8.3   **Slow cities**

The *slow* movement was born in 1999 as a reaction to the frenetic pace of modern life. It is a philosophy that invites us to enjoy the moment and has grown into an international network.

The concept of *slow city* arose in 2006 as part of this trend. Its objective was to improve the quality of life of citizens on the basis of proposals related to the territory, the environment or new technologies. The network is composed of 192 cities in 30 countries.

It is not a quality system, but the participating destinations receive a quality insignia associated with such a lifestyle and ambiance, which itself serves as a form of tourist attraction. These are cities that balance the modern with the traditional. To form part of the network, applicants must meet a series of requisites:

- The application of an environmental policy;

- An urban planning policy to improve the surrounding area, not occupy it;

- The use of technological advances to improve the quality of the environment;

- Encouragement of the production and use of food products produced using natural techniques;

- The protection and development of native production;

- The strengthening of native production;

- Promotion of hospitality and harmonious coexistence between inhabitants and tourists;

- Awareness, both among inhabitants and tourism operators, of what life in a *slow city* means, dedicating special attention to promoting awareness among youth on the basis of specific training plans; and

- A population of no more than 50,000 inhabitants.

Chapter 9

Quality toolkit

Summary   This chapter looks at the tools most commonly used to implement quality.

It analyses the most important tools used in tourism quality systems. It also goes over a few tools that, while not recognized as such, have been key in advancing quality processes in tourism enterprises and destinations.

Key message   There are many kinds of tools available for the improvement of quality, for planning, control, improvement and problem-solving. There are even multifunctional tools. In the case of services, some are more specific than others. In the case of destinations, some are more effective than others.

All can be used to give graphic expression to the data and reasoning behind the analysis and planning of matters affecting the quality of products, services and destinations.

Table 9.1   **A few selected generic quality tools**

Tool	Use			Applicability to		Key tools
	Planning	**Control**	**Improvement**	**Companies**	**Destinations**	
Benchmarking	×		×	×	×	×
Quality Function Deployment (QFD)	×			×	×	×
Brainstorming	×		×	×	×	×
Re-engineering of processes			×	×	×	×
Pareto Diagram		×	×	×	×	
Ishikawa Diagram			×	×	×	×
Flow chart	×			×	×	×
Data collection sheet		×		×	×	×
Gantt Diagram	×	×		×	×	×
Tree diagram	×			×	×	×
P-D-C-A cycle (Plan–Do–Check–Act)	×	×	×	×	×	×
Market studies	×	×	×	×	×	×
Working groups	×		×	×	×	×

9.1   Generic quality tools

Some of the quality tools developed in industrial contexts can be adapted for application to services. New quality techniques have also been developed specifically for services.

9.1.1   Benchmarking

Benchmarking, or comparative evaluation, is the measurement and comparison of some aspect of the activities carried out at a destination with what is observed at other, similar destinations.

It does not require visits to leading destinations, nor does it copy how they do things. It is not an analysis of competitors. It is rather a systematic, structured, formal, analytical and organized process. It is a cooperative methodology.

It is used during the diagnostic assessment of quality to analyse best practices and gather information that could improve a destination's performance. It facilitates the rapid and effective introduction of improvements, by helping to identify barriers and ways to overcome them based on the experience of the destinations studied. Such collaboration raises the level of destinations generally.

All of the leading quality models (Malcolm Baldrige, EFQM, and others) feature benchmarking programmes and some form of comparison with the competition. The entities compared apply a code of ethics in using the shared information.

Once the destinations for comparison have been selected and key processes have been identified, together with related factors, measurements and comparisons are made for the purpose of developing specific improvement plans following the sequence of the P-D-C-A cycle: Plan-Do-Check-Act. Maintaining a common system of indicators will be a great help.

As observed, benchmarking is one of the pillars of the Comprehensive Destination Quality Model (SICTED), in which similarly classified destinations of shared data and address common problems by sharing experiences.

9.1.2   Quality Function Deployment (QFD)

QFD is a method of gathering information about a structured and disciplined process to identify what customers need and want from products and services and make sure they receive it. It has been widely used in the Spanish National Quality Plan as the basis for much of the essential content of its standards and requirements for destinations. It is very useful in defining the characteristics of new products and services.

Methodologically, QFD entails a radical change from the traditional culture of organizations, in that it considers the visitor as the starting and ending point of a process's or product's lifecycle. It entails the systematic use of matrices, as required given the volume of information to be managed and analysed. The QFD systematizes a series of activities that are otherwise incomplete or intuitive and identifies requisites that can be transformed into differentiating advantages.

Its use requires skill. The matrix correlates customer expectations and needs (the what), weighted according to their importance, with the destination's technical requisites and standards (the how). In the case of the Spanish Tourism Quality Plan, this information was gathered by means of surveys. Each cell in the matrix contains a value according to the correlation observed. Adding the values vertically provides the total for each technical requisite. The result is a prioritized ranking of objectives.

Figure 9.1   **Matrix for developing Quality Function Deployment (QFD)**

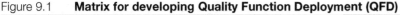
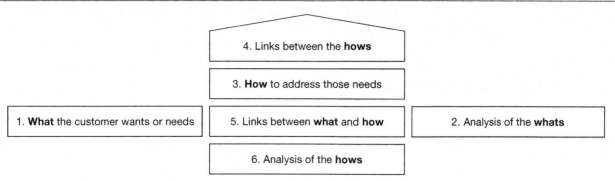

9.1.3   Brainstorming

Brainstorming allows the maximum number of ideas related to a concept to surface spontaneously and collectively and to be gathered for subsequent analysis. It is based on the orderly participation of all involved and the validity in principle of all ideas, with the aim of stimulating group creativity. It is also used in innovation and marketing processes.

Ideas are put forward in an initial phase and then discussed and filtered.

9.1.4   Re-engineering

Re-engineering is the fundamental rethinking and radical redesign of processes to achieve dramatic improvements in critical areas, such as costs, quality, service and speed. It requires the development of a process map to identify potential interactions.

While we have been treating destinations as virtual enterprises, they are not the owners of these processes. The owners are the intervening companies or entities. The processes apply to companies, not destinations. But some processes are the same, depending on the type of destination. For example, the fact that hotels at a ski resort facilitate the purchase of travel packages, provide information about slope conditions and rent equipment, as intermediaries in the process, is similar to the idea of the destination as a virtual enterprise. Hence, adaptation is required in each case.

9.1.5   Pareto Diagram

The Pareto Diagram is a graph consisting of bars organized in descending order and from left to right. It compares the relative importance, and permits prioritization, of all the factors involved in a problem or issue.

It is based on the Pareto Principle, according to which only a few factors are responsible for a determined effect, problem or question. Figure 9.2 below illustrates how the indiscriminate use of capital and small letters, errors in punctuation and incorrect use of fields are the main causes for poor quality in a destination's commercial databases, with a weight of 75%, given the lack of guiding criteria for compilation of the data

Figure 9.2   **Example of a Pareto Diagram**

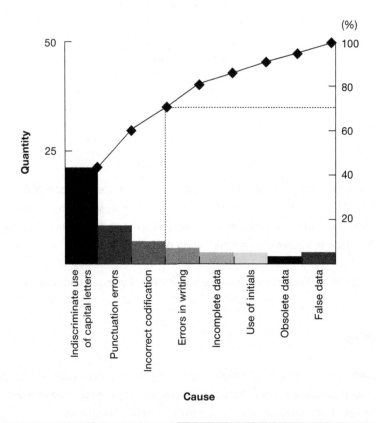

Another example of applying the Pareto Diagram could be the analysis of complaints: not all are equal in terms of recurrence or importance.

9.1.6   Ishikawa Diagram

Given the cross-cutting nature of tourism as activity, the Ishikawa Diagram (also known as the Cause-Effect Diagram or Fish-Bone Diagram because of its shape) is very useful in tourism. It maps the causes and sub-causes that produce a given effect and analyses the logical relationships between them, to facilitate the understanding and analysis of complex problems.

Any phenomenon whose causes are to be identified is an effect, which is written on the right side. A broadly stroked arrow is then placed pointing toward the effect, from left to right.

A deluge of ideas as to possible causes can then be identified and incorporated into the diagram.

To the principle arrow mentioned above, the first- and second-order causes are added. The working group assigned to the process analyses the possible causes identified and circles the most probable, by order of importance, as determined through discussion or voting. The causal chain is then verified. The principal *spines* usually pertain to personnel, materials, procedures, facilities and environment.

Figure 9.3   **Example of an Ishikawa Diagram for a destination in decline**

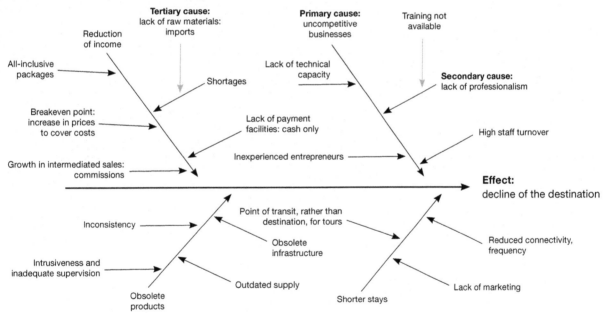

9.1.7   Flow chart

Flowcharts can represent, using standard symbols, the sequences, relationships, responsibilities and expected results of the activities that make up a process. They are also widely used in the design and planning of activities and procedures.

Symbols are used to signify the following:
- Oval: beginning and end of the diagram;
- Rectangle: the execution of one or more activities or procedures;
- Rhombus: issue requiring a decision; alternative;
- Circle: connector of activities to form a procedure;
- Upside down triangle: final file of a document;
- Right side up triangle: temporary file of a document; and
- Arrow: direction or flow of activities.

Figure 9.4   **Example of a flow chart: homemade custard**

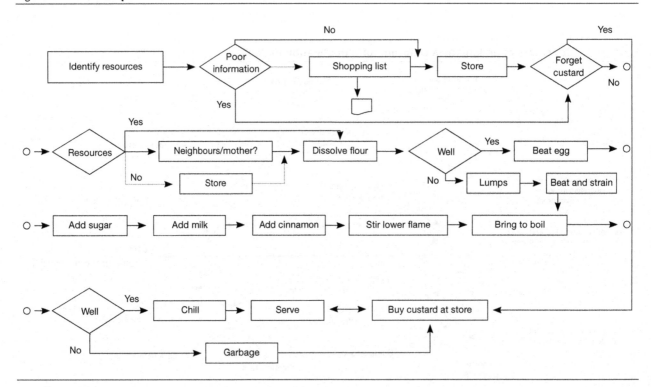

9.1.8   Data collection sheet, survey

A data collection sheet is a record for the orderly and structured gathering of all relevant information. There is no standard format. A good example would be a form for gathering information about the flow of visitors served at information kiosks per day, their nationality and types of inquiry.

9.1.9   Tree diagram

It is a graphic representation that shows the sequence of steps that need to be taken to solve a given situation. The main ideas/concepts branch out into secondary ideas/concepts, and those into a third level and so on to the point considered necessary.

Figure 9.5   **Example of a tree diagram for an airline**

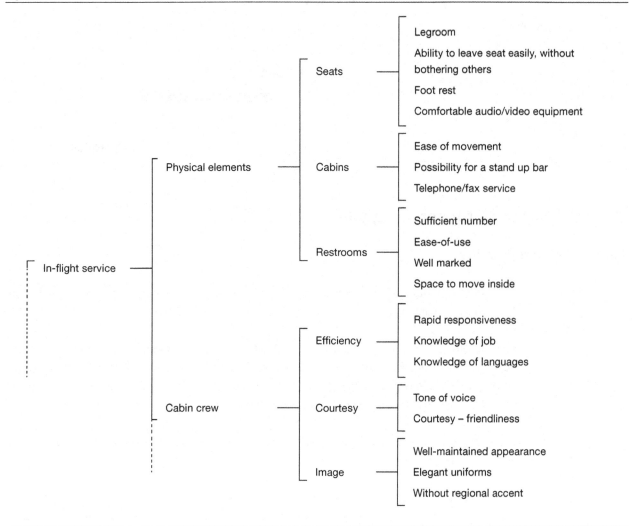

9.1.10   Gantt Diagram

Gantt Diagrams are used to control and monitor projects to verify they are being conducted on schedule, as a tool for improvement. They are used to control complex processes and make optimum use of available resources to complete processes as rapidly as possible by following a critical path. A typical example is a timetable.

Figure 9.6   **Example of a Gantt Diagram: timetable**

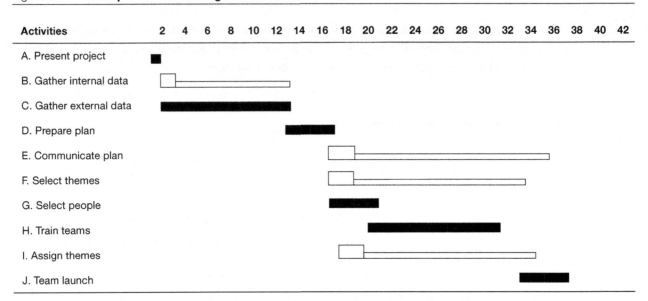

9.2   Other tools for service quality

9.2.1   Working groups

Working groups, not to be confused with quality circles, are one of the main tools for participation. They may be voluntary or not.

Working groups share a same objective, and their structure, responsibility and assigned tasks depend on their capacities. When organized by sector, working groups have common backgrounds and objectives, and work well. In the case of destinations, they are interdisciplinary, their members come from different perspectives, and their projects affect a broader range of interests.

Depending on their duration, groups can have a specific goal, deal with a permanent need, or take charge of an urgent improvement project.

With respect to composition and number of members, there is no ideal criterion: it depends on the nature or priority of the project, the entities to be affected and the availability of people to participate. The synergy derived from the confluence of different bodies of knowledge and skills, enabling teams to achieve results, make it advisable to include at least three or four members. Any fewer would result in an excessive workload for each member, as well as issues of dominance by the strongest member. Large groups, on the other hand, are unwieldy and often break down into subgroups with different and often opposing interests.

Assuming that any quality improvement project relates to an entire process, it is advisable where possible to ensure that domestic suppliers, executing units and the ultimate customers are included in the working group. This is how standard-setting committees are in fact composed, consisting at a minimum of a leader or facilitator and a secretary. If it is not feasible or advisable to include end-users in these groups, arrangements should at least be made to obtain feedback as to potential demand by means of a survey.

The fundamental ingredients for a working group are a clear objective, a need to meet to resolve issues and adherence to a work programme to avoid the counterproductive proliferation of fruitless meetings.

In general, the coexistence of people from different positions within a single working group does not usually affect the dynamic, except in organizations with extremely hierarchical cultures. Proximity to and knowledge of the problem to be addressed, access to information about it and capacity to take immediate action are factors that should be taken into account in selecting group members.

To get any process underway, the agreement must be reached on the projects to be worked on, selected from the possible alternatives, according to their importance, feasibility, foreseeable returns, demonstration effect, positive repercussions among users and cost in time and resources. The implementation of improvement measures will depend on their scope, the priorities established and the level of responsibility of the group members.

There are two interrelated dimensions to working in a group: one is intellectual or technical and the other is emotional. This second dimension can generate *paradigms* or *paradoxes*[1] that need to be interpreted and corrected in order not to reach conclusions or objectives different from those pursued as a consequence of passiveness on the part of certain group members.

Taking into account that destinations are intra-functional, it is impossible to predict the success of any improvement project, however good or timely it might be, without the participation and explicit support of destination actors or individuals intervening in the process. It is precisely on that point – informing, creating interest and involving – where most destination quality initiatives fail. A contributing factor can be an inability to achieve consensus among business and government representatives.

An alternative is therefore to incorporate in the working groups local actors according to their market leadership, rather than simply their representative character. Sometimes institutional representatives participate more out of commitment than conviction and thus become a burden, generating discouragement and ineffectiveness, attitudes that must be avoided at all costs.

Case study 9.1	**Lungau (Austria)**

Lungau is a small Alpine destination in the process of becoming more competitive. Its 15 municipalities have come together to form a single planning body.

To define quality standards and develop new products they have created a working group focused on the quality initiative "New Winter", cataloguing local supply by specialities: hotels for skiers and hotels for hikers, offering related services (equipment rental, information on trail and slope conditions, transport and packages).

---

1   *Paradigm:* phenomenon where working groups develop arguments for discounting information that does not fit into preconceived ideas, as a means of exerting pressure on dissident individuals.
Paradox: process in which members maneuver unconsciously in order to reach situations they do not desire individually but do not oppose out of fear of the group's reaction.

9.2.2   Quality circles

Quality circles are small groups that voluntarily engage in awareness activities, correspondence, quality control, self-development and support in an effort to develop a destination and channel the creative energy of local actors. They form part of the *cultural* aspect of Total Quality, often exchanging experiences inside and outside of the organizations and destination, with the aim of broadening mental horizons and strengthening their own determination. Belief in the effectiveness of quality circles is widespread, but they are not essential.

They are simple to set up but more difficult to maintain over time, given their autonomous character, the resources of all kinds they require and the conditions under which they have to work.

9.2.3   Market studies

Market research is a primary method of obtaining relevant information about the different clienteles for tourism quality, their needs and their perceptions. It is highly advisable to use this method repeatedly.

Studies on-demand help to distinguish client segments; understand their profiles, habits and interests; identify opportunities where needs have not been satisfied; establish the value of the main quality attributes and determine the level of visitor satisfaction with the destination's services, providers and products.

For example, a market study might show that bathrooms are the main indicator of a hotel room's cleanliness. But even if a bathroom is clean, poor lighting, lacklustre and worn porcelain surfaces owing to corrosive cleaning products or blackened joints give an unclean impression. A market study might also lead to the conclusion, for instance, that the Japanese consider any hotel employee, be it a receptionist or bellhop, a legitimate representative for dealing with specific complaints and become frustrated waiting for action without contacting another department. A market study might also conclude that the service most appreciated by business customers, and increasingly by leisure tourists, is a good Internet connection in the room, or that the quality demanded of a destination is inversely proportional to its attractiveness.

Mention must also be made in this connection of *business climate* and *labour climate studies*. The former examine the concerns of business people over market behaviour; the latter, worker satisfaction. They identify sources of conflict and assess behaviour and commitment in relation to defined strategies and decisions conducive to or corrective of various kinds of internal behaviour.

There are different mechanisms for gathering information:
–   **Discussion groups** help to identify and better understand the quality attributes that customers perceive and consider important;
–   **Personal surveys** generate quantitative data for use in identifying the interview subjects' needs, measure their satisfaction and assign weights to quality attributes;
–   **In-depth anthropological interviews:** perceptions are associated with cultural differences based on nationality, recreational interests, etc.;
–   **Panels:** the stable sample provided by a panel permits an examination of how quality initiatives affect individual perceptions; and

- **In-depth interviews:** a good approach for a destination's intermediaries, authorities, business leaders and institutions.

9.2.4 Basic methodological requisites for a survey

Any survey needs to meet certain minimum methodological requirements to make the information obtained representative and useful.

- The *sample,* that is, the group of people interviewed, must be sufficiently representative of the *universe* being studied. If that universe is made up of the visitors to a destination the sample can be established on the basis of type (excursionist/tourist), nationality (outbound markets), season (high or low), sociodemographic profile and age. Another possible criterion is motivation (recreation, business, conference, etc.) group composition (family, friends, individual), form of travel (independent or acquired from a tour operator). In the case of a residents' survey, only the sociodemographic and age profiles will be used.
- The sample's *representative character* needs to be established taking into account *sampling error or estimation error* in the results (the data obtained).
- The *technique* to be used (personal, telephone or online interviews) needs to be selected. Perceptions of service should be inquired about after the service has been used, ideally face-to-face in the airport embarkation room for returning flights, when the customer is *captive.*
- The *moment* must be chosen. The survey should be conducted, using any of the three techniques, once the visitor has returned home. The time lag will make for more even-handed opinions.
- The *type of questions* to be asked must be determined. They may be open-ended or closed. In the latter case the interviewee is asked to choose from several possible answers.

Questions may also refer to a scale of value. In that case, to facilitate measurement, numerical scales (an uneven number) are preferable to semantic ones, which may produce different results depending on cultural and language issues when foreign visitors are interviewed. Alternatively, emojis can be used.

Table 9.2   **Examples of scales in surveys**

Please indicate your satisfaction with the accommodation services during your stay at the destination on a scale of 1 to 7, in which "1" means "not satisfied at all" and "7" means "totally satisfied".

Comfort of the accommodation	Nk/Na	1	2	3	4	5	6	7
Cleanliness and maintenance of the accommodation	Nk/Na	1	2	3	4	5	6	7
Ambience / decor of the establishment	Nk/Na	1	2	3	4	5	6	7

Please assess the quality of accommodation services during your stay at the destination in the following areas:

Comfort	Nk/Na	Extremely poor	Poor	Fair	Good	Excellent
Cleanliness and maintenance	Nk/Na	Extremely poor	Poor	Fair	Good	Excellent
Ambience / decor	Nk/Na	Extremely poor	Poor	Fair	Good	Excellent

Please assess the quality of accommodation services during your stay at the destination in the following areas:

Comfort	Nk/Na	☹	☹	☹	☺	☺
Cleanliness and maintenance	Nk/Na	☹	☹	☹	☺	☺
Ambience / decor	Nk/Na	☹	☹	☹	☺	☺

illustration: © Liluart | Dreamstime.

Note: Nk = Does not know; Na = No answer.

Scales can be useful in defining a value, such as level of satisfaction with a service, product, provider or destination. To establish a reference value in such cases subjects should be questioned separately on the importance attached to different attributes in the market. Participants are usually asked to evaluate a series of attributes summarized in sentences next to a scale, as shown below.

Table 9.3   **Examples of scales in surveys, priority of attributes**

Please react to the following sentences using a scale of 1 to 7, in which 1 means "totally disagree" and 7 means "totally agree".

The destinations are excellent; they appear well-cared-for and harmonious	1	2	3	4	5	6	7
The destinations are excellent; the sites and surroundings are attractive	1	2	3	4	5	6	7
The destinations are excellent; they are very clean	1	2	3	4	5	6	7
The destinations are excellent; they have good signposting	1	2	3	4	5	6	7
The destinations are excellent; they are well organized	1	2	3	4	5	6	7
The destinations are excellent; they are hospitable	1	2	3	4	5	6	7
The destinations are excellent; they have an international airport	1	2	3	4	5	6	7
The destinations are excellent; they are safe/secure	1	2	3	4	5	6	7
The destinations are excellent; they are friendly	1	2	3	4	5	6	7
The destinations are excellent; they are inexpensive	1	2	3	4	5	6	7
The destinations are excellent; they offer a variety of activities for all	1	2	3	4	5	6	7
The destinations are excellent; one can always move about on foot	1	2	3	4	5	6	7
The destinations are excellent; they offer first-rate tourist attractions	1	2	3	4	5	6	7
The destinations are excellent; they always have very friendly reception staff	1	2	3	4	5	6	7
The destinations are excellent; they have multilingual staff	1	2	3	4	5	6	7
The destinations are excellent; they are well connected	1	2	3	4	5	6	7
The destinations are excellent; they have emblematic hotels	1	2	3	4	5	6	7
The destinations are excellent; they offer rich local gastronomy	1	2	3	4	5	6	7
The destinations are excellent; they are located in natural surroundings	1	2	3	4	5	6	7
The destinations are excellent; they are certified	1	2	3	4	5	6	7
The destinations are excellent; they offer comfortable and reliable transport	1	2	3	4	5	6	7
The destinations are excellent; they offer a full range of attractive shops	1	2	3	4	5	6	7

Table 9.4   **Examples of scales in SERVQUAL surveys and evaluation of characteristics according to their importance**

Please select, in the order of their importance, three characteristics that define the excellence of the destination.

	Importance				Importance		
	1°	2°	3°		1°	2°	3°
Well-cared-for, harmonious appearance				One can always move about on foot			
Attractive site and surroundings				First-rate tourist attractions			
Evident cleanliness				Attractive, always friendly personnel			
Good signposting				Multilingual personnel			
Good organization				Good connectivity			
Local hospitality				Emblematic hotels			
International airport				Rich local gastronomy			
Safety and Security				Location in natural surroundings			
Friendliness				Certified			
Inexpensive				Comfortable and reliable transport			
Variety of activities for all				Attractive shops			

To avoid tiring the interviewees and to get the most from their answers the *duration* of the survey is kept short and focused on key aspects of customer satisfaction (from their initial search for information up to the consumption of services and products). If failures are identified the questionnaire can be expanded to inquire about them in greater detail.

The aspects that can be analysed using the different methods indicated vary considerably according to the destination's characteristics. They might include:
–   Citizen security;
–   Pollution (noise, visual or environmental);
–   Quality/price ratio;
–   Order and surroundings;
–   Traffic, public transport and parking;
–   Cleanliness;
–   Natural resource conservation;
–   Hospitality;
–   Professionalism and language skills; and
–   Adequacy of receptive infrastructure, among others.

Comparisons can be drawn with some competing destination the customers may have visited previously. It should be remembered that expectations and satisfaction are subjective factors that depend on each individual, so comparisons will need to be adjusted.

Table 9.5　　**Examples of comparative questions for a destination satisfaction survey**

Please indicate how this city compares with [the cities or areas mentioned].

	Much worse	Worse	The same	Better	Much better	Nk/Na
Tourist attractions	1	2	3	4	5	/
Tourism services and infrastructure	1	2	3	4	5	/
Security/health/hygiene	1	2	3	4	5	/
Quality/price ratio	1	2	3	4	5	/

Note:　　Nk = Does not know; Na = No answer.

Table 9.6　　**Examples of questions to assess satisfaction with a destination's services**

	1	2	3	4	5	6	7	8	9	10	Nk/Na

Please indicate your level of satisfaction with the following aspects of your trip and stay in this city on a scale of 1 to 10, where 1 means "totally dissatisfied" and 10 "totally satisfied"

What is your level of satisfaction with…?

	1	2	3	4	5	6	7	8	9	10	Nk/Na
Tourist attractions in this place/area	1	2	3	4	5	6	7	8	9	10	/
Tourist excursions and activities	1	2	3	4	5	6	7	8	9	10	/
Your guide/tourism personnel	1	2	3	4	5	6	7	8	9	10	/
Recreation and entertainment options	1	2	3	4	5	6	7	8	9	10	/
Accommodation/hotel	1	2	3	4	5	6	7	8	9	10	/
Food in restaurants/hotels	1	2	3	4	5	6	7	8	9	10	/
Transport	1	2	3	4	5	6	7	8	9	10	/
Shopping	1	2	3	4	5	6	7	8	9	10	/

On the same scale of 1 to 10, where 1 means "totally dissatisfied" and 10 "totally satisfied" how satisfied are you with the following aspects of this city?

Accessibility to the destination

	1	2	3	4	5	6	7	8	9	10	Nk/Na
Frequency of transport services to this city	1	2	3	4	5	6	7	8	9	10	/
Ticket prices	1	2	3	4	5	6	7	8	9	10	/
Immigration formalities (for the country concerned)	1	2	3	4	5	6	7	8	9	10	/

Excursions offered

	1	2	3	4	5	6	7	8	9	10	Nk/Na
Excursions and recreation available in this place/area is broad, varied, attractive	1	2	3	4	5	6	7	8	9	10	/
The information provided is accurate, detailed, complete	1	2	3	4	5	6	7	8	9	10	/
Good quality/price ratio	1	2	3	4	5	6	7	8	9	10	/

	1	2	3	4	5	6	7	8	9	10	Nk/Na
The excursions and recreational activities are well planned and organized	1	2	3	4	5	6	7	8	9	10	/
The number of participants is appropriate	1	2	3	4	5	6	7	8	9	10	/
The recreational activities and entertainment offered											
The supply is broad and varied	1	2	3	4	5	6	7	8	9	10	/
There are quality actitivities	1	2	3	4	5	6	7	8	9	10	/
The atmosphere is friendly	1	2	3	4	5	6	7	8	9	10	/
Transport											
Punctuality	1	2	3	4	5	6	7	8	9	10	/
Cleanliness	1	2	3	4	5	6	7	8	9	10	/
Safety/security	1	2	3	4	5	6	7	8	9	10	/
Fair price	1	2	3	4	5	6	7	8	9	10	/
Tourism personnel/guides											
Quality of information provided	1	2	3	4	5	6	7	8	9	10	/
Accessibility, attentiveness, friendliness	1	2	3	4	5	6	7	8	9	10	/
Professionalism and language ability	1	2	3	4	5	6	7	8	9	10	/
Optimal attention to incidents and complaints	1	2	3	4	5	6	7	8	9	10	/
Accommodation											
Appearance and decor	1	2	3	4	5	6	7	8	9	10	/
Cleanliness, maintenance	1	2	3	4	5	6	7	8	9	10	/
Professionalism, reliability and efectiveness of staff	1	2	3	4	5	6	7	8	9	10	/
Restaurant food											
Tastiness, quality	1	2	3	4	5	6	7	8	9	10	/
Professionalism, efficiency of service	1	2	3	4	5	6	7	8	9	10	/
Décor is warm	1	2	3	4	5	6	7	8	9	10	/
Wide range of local/native cuisine	1	2	3	4	5	6	7	8	9	10	/

Note: Nk = Does not know; Na = No answer.

List of acronyms and abbreviations

AENOR	Asociación Española de Normalización
	(Spanish Association for Standardisation and Certification)
	Note: In 2017, the activities of AENOR (Asociación Española de Normalización) have been divided into two bodies: (1) The Asociación Española de Normalización – UNE (Spanish Association for Stardardisation), carrying out standardisation and certification activities; and (2) AENOR, a commercial entity which works in the field of conformity assessment and other related areas, such as training and the sales of publications.
CEN	European Committee for Standardization
CNTA	China National Tourism Administration
CODEMA	Comisión para el Desarrollo de la Zona Metropolitana de Acapulco
	(Commission for the Development of Greater Acapulco)
CTN	Comités Técnicos de Normalización
	(Technical Standardization Committees [Spain])
DMO	Destination management organization
EDEN	European Destinations of Excellence
EFQM	European Foundation for Quality Management
EMAS	EU-Eco Management and Audit Scheme
EU	European Union
FEDECATUR	Federación de Cámaras de Turismo de Centroamérica
	(Central American Federation of Chambers of Tourism)
ICTE	Instituto para la Calidad Turística Española
	(Institute for Spanish Tourism Quality)
ISO	International Organization for Standardization
NTO	National tourism organization
P-D-C-A	Plan–Do–Check–Act
QFD	Quality Function Deployment
RevPAR	Revenue per available room
SGS	Société Générale de Surveillance
SICTED	Sistema Integral de Calidad Turística en Destinos
	(Comprehensive Destination Quality Model [Spain])
SME	Small and medium-sized enterprises
TGCSA	Tourism Grading Council of South Africa
UNE	Una Norma Española (A Spanish Standard)
UNESCO	United Nations Educational, Scientific and Cultural Organization
UNWTO	World Tourism Organization
USAID	United States Agency for International Development

WHO   World Health Organization
WTTC   World Travel & Tourism Council

Glosary

Accreditation: voluntary process through which an organization is able to measure the quality of its services or products and their performance relative to recognized standards.

Audit: systematic and objective activity to determine the degree to which requisites associated with the matters to be covered by the audit have been complied with. Audits are conducted by one or more independent persons with no involvement in the matters to be audited.

Brainstorming: tool enabling a group to generate numerous ideas and present them in an orderly fashion.

Cause-effect diagram: tool to help identify, classify and bring to light the possible causes of a phenomenon, whether it be a specific problem or a factor generally conducive to quality. It illustrates graphically the relationships that exist between a given result (effect) and the factors (causes) contributing to that result.

Certification: process through which a duly accredited entity confirms the capacity of a company or product to meet the requirements of a standard.

Checklist: is a printed sheet in table or diagram format in which data are recorded and compiled using a simple and systematic method, such as checkmarks, to signify that determined steps have occurred.

Complaint: expression of dissatisfaction with a service or product.

Consensus: decision taken by a group that is accepted by all members without taking a vote. All members support the decision even if there is not total agreement.

Continuous improvement: systematic, planned process to improve the services, products, processes and results of an organization.

Control centre/dashboard: document showing key indicators for the control of management at the desired level, whether departmental or business wide, or, in the case of public administrations, at the level of an administrative unit, the jurisdiction of a municipality, an institution or an entire organization.

Costs of lack of quality: resources and efforts expended by an organization that add no value to the activity and thus represent a cost.

Costs of prevention: expenses dedicated by an organization to avoiding mistakes. These are costs derived from the actions that help the organization, its departments, units and employees do their work well the first time.

Costs of quality: costs derived from the effort dedicated by an organization to preventing errors or evaluating processes and their results.

Costs owing to external failures: costs associated with the defects found after the product or service has been delivered to the customer.

Costs owing to internal failures: costs incurred by the organization as a result of errors committed in its processes and activities but detected before the product or service is delivered to the customer.

Customer: person, organization or process that receives products or services from a provider.

Customer voice: method of determining and systematizing the quality requisites (demanded quality) based on direct contact with the different market segments, to establish what quality factors contribute most decisively to making the product or service satisfactory.

Effectiveness: degree to which planned activities achieve expected results.

Efficiency: relationship between the result achieved and the resources used.

Environment: the surroundings of the place in which an organization operates, including the air, water, soil, natural resources, flora, fauna, human beings and their interaction.

Environmental impact: any change in environment, adverse or beneficial, total or partial, that derives from the activities, products or services of an organization.

Environmental management system: that part of the overall management system that includes the organizational structure, planning activities, responsibilities, practices, procedures, processes and resources used it to develop, implement, realize, review and maintain environmental policy.

Expectation: what the customer expects from a product or service.

Expected quality: what the customer needs, requires and expects, as expressed more or less explicitly. This represents real quality, the objective to be achieved.

Flowchart: a diagram that uses symbols to represent the flow and phases of a process and that is especially useful at the start of a plan to improve processes, to show how the plan will unfold. A basic tool for the management of processes.

Gantt Diagram: used to control and monitor projects to verify that they are being conducted as scheduled.

Generic competencies: crosscutting professional competencies that are transferable to different functions and tasks.

Globalization: process tending toward increased integration of economies throughout the world, especially through trade and financial flows, as a result of human innovation and technological progress.

Indicator: magnitude associated with a characteristic of a result, process, activity, structure, etc., permitting a regular evaluation of the characteristics and fulfilment of established objectives (standards) through successive measurements and comparison with an established standard.

Internal customer: member of an organization receiving the result of a previous process conducted within the same organization which can be considered to form part of an internal network of providers and customers.

Internal communication: body of verbal and non-verbal messages transmitted within the framework of an organization.

Ishikawa Diagram: a map of the causes and sub-causes contributing to a given effect for the purpose of analysing how they inter-relate and thus better understanding complex problems.

Key processes: processes used to manage the activities that go into delivering a product or service to the customer. They form part of an organization's mission and generally consume most of its resources.

Labour climate: organizational quality or characteristics perceived by the members of an organization that influence their behaviour.

Leadership: process of social influence by which the leader gains the voluntary participation of subordinates in pursuit of the organization's objectives.

Map of processes: diagram of an organization's processes and how they interrelate.

Mission: an organization's reason for being; what characterizes it and differentiates it from others, and guides the efforts and actions of its members.

Motivation: what drives a person to act in a particular way. This drive to action, whether external or internal, provokes a state of need that breaks the internal balance and causes dissatisfaction and tension for the individual, who feels the need to act so as to reestablish the internal balance. If the behaviour is effective, the individual will feel that the need has been satisfied.

Need: something that is required by an individual and that motivates action to satisfy it.

Non-conformity: failure to comply with a requisite for a process that may relate to many things, such as service that does not meet the customer's needs, an operation or activity not in accordance with the procedure provided in the Procedures Manual or the performance of an administrative formality through unofficial channels.

Organization: consciously coordinated social unit composed of two or more individuals functioning in a relatively continuous manner in order to achieve a shared goal or set of goals.

Pareto Diagram: method of analysis consisting of a figure permitting the most important causes of a problem (the few that are truly vital) to be distinguished from the less important ones (the many and the trivial).

Procedure: specific way of performing an activity or process.

Process: set of interrelated activities that transform one or more inputs into an output (result).

Productivity: measure of the efficiency of an organization in terms of products obtained from resources used (productivity = products/factors).

Professional competency: effective exercise of capacities in the performance of an occupation up to the levels required. It is more than technical knowledge, in terms of knowing, and knowing how to do things, since it also encompasses the behaviours considered necessary to fully exercise an occupation, which include capacity for analysis, decision-making, transmission of information, etc.

Programmed quality: quality that is being pursued, and which has therefore been the object of planning.

Protocol: orderly sequence of actions that need to be taken in a given situation.

Quality (according to ISO 8402): the totality of characteristics of a product or service that bear upon its ability to satisfy stated and implied needs.

Quality assurance: a set of planned and systematic activities applied to a quality system in order for the quality requisites of a product or service to be satisfied.

Quality control: system of technical activities to measure the attributes and performance of a process, product or service relative to certain defined standards, to verify whether they meet established requisites.

QFD: Quality Function Deployment: methodology for systematizing information obtained from the customer so as to define the characteristics of quality service and adapted to the needs and expectations detected. It therefore provides a tool for design of the product or service. It was introduced in Japan by Yoji Akao in 1966.

Quality improvement: an aspect of quality management concerned with building capacity for meeting quality requisites.

Quality management: range of management activities, performed as general functions, that determine quality policy, objectives and responsibilities in the context of a quality system.

Quality plan: document specifying the procedures and corresponding resources to be applied in implementing a quality system for a project, product or process, as well as the actors and amounts of time required.

Quality planning: the part of quality management concerned with establishing quality objectives and the operational processes and resources necessary to reach those objectives.

Quality policy: a set of general directives and instructions with respect to quality formally issued by the senior management of an organization.

Quality service: accessory aspects to the principle service being provided, to enrich it and better satisfy customer needs and expectations.

Quality system: series of coordinated activities relating to the set of elements (resources, procedures, documents, organizational structure and strategies) required to achieve quality in products or services.

Realized quality: quality that truly results from an organization's activity.

Redesign of processes: critical analysis of the processes that, from the perspective of continuous improvement and by modifying the content and sequence of activities, lead to improvements in what is referred to as quality, including time savings, customer satisfaction and/or cost-reduction.

Re-engineering: fundamental review and radical redesign of processes in order to achieve spectacular improvements in critical and contemporaneous performance indicators, with respect to costs, quality, service, speed, etc.

Requisite: established need or expectation, generally implicit or obligatory.

Self-evaluation: process carried out by an organization to identify strengths and areas for improvement.

Standardization: collective activity for the purpose of developing solutions to repetitive situations. Entails the development, dissemination and application of standards.

Strategic planning: process of conceiving a desirable future and defining the means to realize it.

Synergy: combined action of two or more causes in which the whole is greater than the sum of the parts. Synergy exists when the result or objective achieved is greater than what is achieved by adding up what is contributed by each of the parts.

Team: organized group of people working together to achieve a goal.

Technical competencies: professional skills directly related to an occupation, non transferable to other functions or tasks. They might also be referred to as "specific competencies"

Tree diagram: technique that provides an overview of the means necessary to achieve a goal or solve a problem.

Turnover: fluctuation in the personnel of an organization. Also refers to the number of people joining and leaving a company.

Values: essential, lasting principles of an organization. A set of principles to guide employee behaviour and attitudes in an organization.

Vision: purpose to be accomplished in the future and to which the organization is dedicated.

References and bibliography

Almeida, A.; **Barcos,** M.; **Redín,** L. and **Martín Castilla,** J. (2006), *Gestión de la Calidad de los procesos turísticos,* Síntesis, Madrid.

Álvarez Sousa, A. (2003), *Turismo y calidad global. Contribución al desarrollo integral. La Calidad Integral del Turismo,* V Congreso de Turismo Universidad y Empresa, Tirant lo Blanch, Valencia.

Assaf, G. and **Tsionas,** E. (2015), 'Incorporating destination quality into the measurement of tourism performance: A Bayesian approach', *International Journal of Tourism Management,* number 49.

Berry, L. L. and **Parasuraman,** A. (1993), *Marketing de Servicios: La Calidad como meta,* Parramón, Barcelona.

Blanquer Criado, D. V. (2003), *La calidad integral del turismo, La Calidad Integral del Turismo,* V Congreso de Turismo Universidad y Empresa, Tirant lo Blanch, Valencia.

Boniface, P. (2013), *Managing Quality Cultural Tourism,* Routledge, Oxford, Google eBook.

Boullón, R. (2003), *Calidad turística en la pequeña y mediana empresa,* Ediciones Turísticas, Madrid.

Bravo, O. and **Senlle,** A. (1997), *ISO 9000 en la práctica – La calidad en el sector turístico,* Ediciones Gestión 2000, Madrid.

Buttle, F. (1996), 'SERVQUAL: review, critique, research agenda', *European Journal of Marketing,* volume 30, Manchester Business School, Manchester.

Carrasco, S. (2013), *Procesos de gestión de calidad en hostelería y turismo,* Paraninfo, Madrid.

Chaves Garita, D. (1999), *Memoria del Taller Regional de Certificación y Sellos para el Turismo en Centroamérica,* PROARCA/CAPAS, CCAD, San José.

Chen, Y.; **Zhang,** H. and **Qiu,** L. (2012), *A Review on Tourist Satisfaction of Tourism Destinations,* LISS 2012, Springer, Berlin.

Crosby, P. (1996), *Reflexiones sobre Calidad,* McGraw Hill Interamericana Editores S.A. de C.V., Mexico City.

Diaz-Perez, F. M. (2010), *Competitive Strategies and Policies for Tourism Destinations,* Nova Science Publishers Inc., New York.

European Commission (2003), *A Manual for Evaluating the Quality Performance of Tourist Destinations and Services,* Office for Official Publications of the European Communities, Luxembourg.

European Commission (2000), *Integrated quality management (IQM) of coastal tourist destinations,* Office for Official Publications of the European Communities, Luxembourg.

European Commission (2000), *Integrated quality management (IQM) of rural tourist destinations,* Office for Official Publications of the European Communities, Luxembourg.

European Commission (2000), *Integrated quality management (IQM) for urban tourist destinations,* Office for Official Publications of the European Communities, Luxembourg.

Gálgano, A. (1995), *Los siete instrumentos de la Calidad Total,* Editorial Díaz de Santos, Madrid.

Go, F. M. and **Govers,** R. (2014), 'Integrated quality management for tourist destinations: a European perspective on achieving competitiveness', *Tourism Management,* number 21.

Gorga, V. (1999), 'Una aproximación a la calidad turística en el plano internacional', *Revista de Estudios Turísticos.*

Granados Cabezas, V. (1999), *La gestión de la Calidad en el municipio turístico,* Junta de Andalucía, Sevilla.

Heart of England Tourist Board (1989), *Quality first,* Heart of England Tourist Board.

Jennings, G. (2006), *Quality tourism experiences,* Elsevier, London.

Jones, E. and **Haven-Tang,** C. (2005), *Tourism SMES, Service Quality and Destination Competitiveness,* Cab International, Wallingford.

Keane, M. T. (2010), 'Sustaining quality in tourism destinations: an economic model with an application', *Aplied Economics,* number 28, Routledge, Oxford.

Keller, P. (1997), *Quality management in tourism,* Congress of International Association of Scientific Experts in Tourism, AIEST.

Kim, J. (2014), 'The antecedents of memorable tourism experiences: the development of a scale to measure the destination attributes associated with memorable experiences', *International Journal of Tourism Management,* number 44.

Kim, S. and **Holland,** S. (2013), 'A Structural Model for Examining how Destination Image, Perceived Value, and Service Quality Affect Destination Loyalty: a Case Study of Orlando', *International Journal of Tourism Research,* number 15.

Langer, M. (1997), *Service Quality in Tourism: Measurement Methods and Empirical Analysis,* Peter Lang International Publishers, Pieterlen.

Lenehan, T. (1998), *Managing quality in tourism: theory and practice,* Oak Tree Press, Dublin.

Llamas, Ch. (2009), *Marketing y gestión de calidad turística,* Liber Factory, Madrid.

Martínez, I. and **Salanova Soria,** M. (2000), *Percepciones sobre Calidad de servicio en el sector turístico de la Comunidad Valenciana: un estudio cualitativo,* II Congreso universidad y empresa, Tirant lo Blanch, Valencia.

Miguel Dávila, J. A. (2002), *Calidad del Servicio en el Sector Turístico,* Netbiblo, A Coruña.

Mok, C.; **Sparks,** B. and **Kadampully,** J. (2001), *Service Quality Management in Hospitality, Tourism, and Leisure,* Routledge, Oxford.

Moutinho, L. and **Albayrak,** T. (2011), 'How Far does Overall Service Quality of a Destination Affect Clients' Post-Purchase Behaviours?', *International Journal of Tourism Research,* number 14.

Murphy, P. (1996), *Quality Management in Urban Tourism,* Wiley, New York.

Otero, S. (2002), 'Los aspectos socio-culturales como factores de identificación para la gestión de calidad del turismo rural, Jalisco, México', *II Foro Mundial de Turismo Rural,* Universidad de Guadalajara and Universidad Nacional del Litoral, Jalisco.

Parasuraman, A.; **Zeithaml,** V. A. and **Berry,** L. L. (1992), *Calidad total en la gestión de servicios,* Editorial Díaz de Santos, Madrid.

Parasuraman, A.; **Zeithaml,** V. A. and **Berry,** L. L. (1991), 'Perceived Service Quality as a Client-Based Performance Measure: An Empirical Examination of Organizational Barriers Using an Extended Service Quality Mode', *Human Resource Management.*

Parasuraman, A.; **Zeithaml,** V. A. and **Berry,** L. L. (1988), 'SERVQUAL a Multiple-Item Scale for Measuring Consumer Perceptions of Service Quality', *Journal of Retailing,* volume 64 (1), spring, pp. 5–6 and 12–40.

Parasuraman, A.; **Zeithaml,** V. A. and **Berry,** L. L. (1985), 'A Conceptual Model of Service Quality and its Implications for Future Research', *Journal of Marketing,* volume 49, autumn, pp. 41–50.

Pearce, P. L. (2005), *Tourist Behaviour: Themes and Conceptual Schemes,* Channel View Publications, Bristol.

Peters, T. (2002), *Reinventando el trabajo: las claves de la productividad,* Nowtilus.

Pulido, J. I. and **Navarro,** U. (2014), *Identificación de ítems para medir las experiencias del turista en destino,* Revista Cultur, year 8 (1), Ilhéus-Bahia.

Ramirez Cavassa, C. (2002), *Calidad total en las empresas turisticas/ Total Quality in the Tourism Business,* Trillas, Mexico City.

Rust, R. T.; **Zahorik,** A. J. and **Keiningham,** T. L. (1995), 'Return on quality: Making service quality financially accountable', *Journal of Marketing.*

Scott, N. and **Laws,** E. (2013), *Knowledge Sharing and Quality Assurance in Hospitality and Tourism,* Routledge, Oxford/Google eBook.

Secretaría de Turismo, Gobierno de México (2013), *Breviario de cultura turística,* SECTUR, Mexico City.

Shlesinger, L. A. and **Heskett,** J. L. (1997), *Service Profit Chain,* Simon and Schuster.

Stredel Laurent, A. (2005), 'Calificación, clasificación y comercialización del turismo rural', *Seminario Internacional de Turismo Rural,* Armenia, Quindío, Memorias.

Valls, J. F. (2000), Gestión de empresas de turismo, *El arte de provocar satisfacción,* Gestión 2000, Barcelona.

Vázquez Casielles, R. and **Díaz Martín,** A. M. (1995), *Calidad de Servicio en el Turismo Rural,* V Congreso Nacional de Economía, Economía de los Servicios, Las Palmas de Gran Canaria.

Veasnaa, S.; **Wub,** W. and **Huanga,** Ch. (2013), 'The impact of destination source credibility on destination satisfaction: The mediating effects of destination attachment and destination image', *International Journal of Tourism Research,* number 36.

Weiermair, K. and **Peters,** M. (2012), *Quality-of-Life Values Among Stakeholders in Tourism Destinations: A Tale of Converging and Diverging Interests and Conflicts,* International Handbooks of Quality-of-Life.

Williams, C. and **Buswell,** J. (2003), *Service Quality in Leisure and Tourism,* Cab International, Wallingford.

World Health Organization (2011), *World report on disability 2011,* WHO, Geneva.

World Health Organization (1980), *International Classification of Impairments, Disabilities, and Handicaps: Manual for classifying the consequences,* WHO, Geneva.

World Tourism Organization, ONCE Foundation and **European Network for Accessible Tourism** (2016), *Manual on Accessible Tourism for All: Principles, Tools and Best Practices,* modules I and V available in English, UNWTO, Madrid.

World Tourism Organization, ONCE Foundation and **European Network for Accessible Tourism** (2014 and 2015), *Manual de Turismo Accesible para Todos – Principios, herramientas y buenas prácticas,* modules I to V available in Spanish, UNWTO, Madrid.

World Tourism Organization and **ACS Foundation** (2014), *Manual on Accessible Tourism for All: Public-Private Partnerships and Good Practices,* UNWTO, Madrid.

World Tourism Organization (2012), *Toolbox for Crisis Communications in Tourism – Checklists and best practices,* UNWTO, Madrid.

World Tourism Organization (2010), *Normas y sistemas de calidad en el turismo y su relación con la sostenibilidad y las leyes de turismo – La experiencia de las Américas,* UNWTO, Madrid.

World Tourism Organization (2005), *Tourism Congestion Management at Natural and Cultural Sites – A Guidebook,* UNWTO, Madrid.

World Tourism Organization (2003), *UNWTO Quality Support Committee at its sixth meeting,* Varadero, Cuba, 9–10 May 2003, UNWTO, Madrid.

World Tourism Organization (2001), *Pulbic-Private Sector Cooperation – Enhancing Tourism Competitiveness,* UNWTO, Madrid.

World Tourism Organization (1980), *Manila Declaration on World Tourism,* UNWTO, Manila.

Yuan, Y. (2014), *Quality evaluation of tourism service based on multi-level grey theory? A case study of Zhangjiajie city,* 11th International Conference on Service Systems and Service Management.

Zapata, M. J . and **Hall,** M. (2012), 'Public-private collaboration in the tourism sector: balancing legitimacy and effectiveness in local tourism partnership', *Journal of Policy Reseach in Tourism, Leisure and Events,* volume 4 (1), Routledge (online), available in: http://dx.doi.org/10.1080/19407963.2011.634069 (25-05-2015).

Zeithaml, V. A and **Bitner,** M. J. (2012), *Services Marketing,* McGraw-Hill, New York.

Technical tourism journals:

Annals of Tourism Research

www.journals.elsevier.com/annals-of-tourism-research/ (28-05-2015).

International Tourism Quarterly

Journal of Hospitality and Travel Research

Revista de Estudios Turísticos

www.iet.tourspain.es/es-ES/documentacionturistica/ revistaestudiosturisticos/Paginas/default.aspx.

Tourism Review

www.aiest.org/publications/tourism-review/.

Lightning Source UK Ltd.
Milton Keynes UK
UKOW07f1638170817
307487UK00002B/41/P

9 789284 417971